WINNING
THE
FIGHT
TO BE
HAPPY

WINNING
THE
FIGHT
TO BE
HAPPY

*Strategies to overcome negativity,
depression, and other internal struggles*

TOM McKINLEY

iUniverse

WINNING THE FIGHT TO BE HAPPY
Strategies to overcome negativity, depression, and other internal struggles

iUniverse books may be ordered through booksellers or by contacting:

iUniverse
1663 Liberty Drive
Bloomington, IN 47403
www.iuniverse.com
1-800-Authors (1-800-288-4677)

ISBN: 978-1-4917-8409-9 (sc)
ISBN: 978-1-4917-8408-2 (e)

Library of Congress Control Number: 2015920088

Print information available on the last page.

iUniverse rev. date: 02/23/2016

Back cover photograph courtesy of Michael Burns

TABLE OF CONTENTS

For my family and friends, without whom neither this book nor myself would be here.

No one makes it alone.

INTRODUCTION

Our life is a warfare, and a mere pilgrimage.
– Marcus Aurelius

Some people are born happy; others have to fight for it. This book is for the latter.

When I was 20, a friend described me as "happy go lucky." Ten years later, I found myself on the brink of a depression that was to last for the majority of my 30s. It crippled me professionally, put friendships at risk, and made romantic relationships impossible. In a short amount of time, I had become a person who was lost and hopeless.

As I looked deeper into myself, I realized that my depression was based less on external events and more on the person that I was inside. The seeds of my unhappiness had always been present in my mind. It had just taken a few disappointments to make them grow.

My depression was worsened by my natural anxiety issues, but even more so by a streak of negativity that I had always carried with me. I had always thought that I viewed my life objectively, when really I was a complete pessimist. The combination of these elements put me into a downward spiral – or perhaps more accurately, a plunge. My life simply got worse and worse.

I finally saw that I owed it to myself to fight against this with every resource I had, as well as with every resource I could find. In this process, I discovered a wealth of ways to deal with my depression and negativity. One result is that I am now a happy person, with an inner reservoir of peace of mind, and an outlook on life that is both optimistic and realistic. Another result is this book, in which I'll tell you what worked for me and what can work for you.

You can think of this book as a map, a diagram, or whatever you wish. I myself think of it as a guide. The path to peace of mind and happiness is rocky and full of pitfalls. Life is an ongoing sequence of conflict and confrontation, of moments that comprise the full spectrum from happiness to suffering. Whatever life may be, it is not, in itself, peaceful. It is, as Marcus Aurelius says above, a warfare. And hence I do not try to tell you that you will get happier by simply *believing* in peace and positivity. To get happier, you will need to learn how to fight against the forces of negativity, and how to win. In this learning process, you will empower yourself, developing inner peace and a positive perspective.

⚜

Winning the Fight to Be Happy is a product of my realization that I was not alone in suffering anxiety, overthinking, self-hatred, and ultimately depression. I had always thought that I was the "weird one," that everyone around me was happy except myself -- but I was wrong. Knowing this did not make me any happier, but it certainly motivated me to start writing.

This is also a book about the dangers of negative thinking. I have never met a happy person who had a negative perspective. Happy people think positively. For some, it is easy: they are born that way. For others – including myself and those reading this book – a positive perspective is something that has to be fought for and cultivated. That's what I am here for.

One term that you will see over and over again in this book is "Tunnel Vision." This term refers to the state of negativity that we find ourselves in, in which we see everything through our own limited and negative perspective. Unfortunately, because we are in a "tunnel," we don't see that there are alternatives, and we don't even realize where we are. Getting you out of that tunnel is my job.

I have written this book in a holistic manner, by which I mean that all chapters are interrelated. While there is a progression, feel free to jump in anywhere – there's no need to start at the beginning. Many of the same topics and strategies arise throughout, and you will be amazed at how simple solutions apply to a variety of problems. I also quote from people of wisdom, whose words have stood the test of time. Many of the quotes are from 2,000 years ago – proof that the path to happiness has not changed much over the years.

BEFORE WE START

Just a quick note before we start: I will never make any suggestion unless it has personally worked for me, or for someone with whom I am very close (and in such cases, I will be sure to make it clear). I don't believe in tossing theories around to see if they will work or not. You want to get better, starting today, and the best way to do that is for me to tell you strategies that really work.

Another principle: I will be totally honest about myself, as long as you remain honest with yourself while reading this book. Let down your guard, and just read and feel. When you want to question, please question. But bear in mind that this is not written as an academic treatise. The goal of reading this book is to feel better about yourself and your life.

So let's begin. I look forward to our journey together.

1 CHANGE

I'll begin with a major theme of this book, and one which is essential to grasp if you want to put yourself on the path to happiness and peace of mind: Change. Right now, your opinion of it is probably not very positive. But it is the first step to take in making yourself a happier person.

When Ben Franklin said that two things were certain in life – death and taxes -- he omitted to mention Change. Change is written into the DNA of life.

> *Change is written into the DNA of life.*

"All things are change, yet we need not fear anything new," says Marcus Aurelius, whom I first quoted in the Introduction. Reigning at the height of the Roman Empire, Aurelius was a man who dealt with pressing issues on a daily basis, and he accepted change as a part of life that could be looked at with optimism. The more positive you become, the more you too will accept change, as you will realize that it often brings positive things. A sheer dislike of change is a symptom of negative people.

There are two types of change: internal and external. That is, there are changes we initiate ourselves, and changes which happen outside of our control.

What we are mainly concerned with in this chapter is internal change: the kind you have control over. Jack Welch, CEO of GE, used to tell his employees, "Change or die." This is a bit extreme for our purposes, but we can admit that common sense tells us that if something is not working, you need to change what is being done about it.

During one of the most difficult periods of my life, I woke up one day in my hot, claustrophobic apartment, and BAM! The full awfulness of my life situation hit me. It had been a terrible year: money, my job, problems with friendships and relationships, you name it. And in thinking about all these things, over and over, for the millionth time, I finally "lost it" – I pounded the walls, swore, and shouted. I always thought that foaming at the mouth was something that only happened in cartoons, but I found out that it was real! And when I calmed down and sank to the floor in exhaustion and shame, the conclusion I came to was that something had to change. I waited and waited.

And waiting was the problem. For years, I went through my life expecting the circumstances around me to magically improve. At the same time, I disliked the concept of change. In short, I wanted my life to get better without actually changing. It was irrational, and I was expecting the impossible. Throughout all of this, it never occurred to me that the things that needed to change were inside my own head. I had a tendency to overthink, I drank too much, I read books that entertained me but which didn't teach me anything about how to improve my life – just to name a few of my shortcomings. And when this approach didn't work, do you know what I did? I blamed luck, my IQ, the weather, the economy, my past – not once did I attribute it to my refusal to move with the current, and accept that I needed to make some serious changes.

In order to write this book, I had to change. I had to wake up early to find time to write, and I had to work around a busy job and part-time jobs. If I had kept on living life the way I did several years ago, I would be just as unhappy, and this book would never have been written.

THE BEGINNINGS OF CHANGE

Where can you start making changes? When you want your life to improve, you start by looking at your daily activities and routines, no matter how "ordinary." Look at what is

> *When you want your life to improve, you start by looking at your daily activities and routines, no matter how "ordinary."*

healthy, and what is not. You'll be surprised at how many minor things accumulate into being harmful to your progress.

I used to insist on watching at least one movie per day, a DVD, after dinner; and often, if I enjoyed it, I would watch another. Then, on top of having spent four hours staring at the TV screen, I'd get to sleep late and not be fresh for the morning. While watching the films, I'd have more than a few drinks. In the morning I'd be dehydrated and hung over, and not in the mood for going to work.

The first change I made was making sure to get a good night's sleep. It was basic: if I was tired all the time, there was no way I could do my best at work or look for new opportunities. What made matters worse was that I was a poor sleeper, often waking up several times during the night, as well as before my alarm clock. I saw a doctor about this, and his advice was simple: "Tom, if you need more hours of sleep, go to bed earlier." I made sure I was in bed by 10 pm, and almost immediately, I started to begin each day with more energy and more positivity. The fact that I was able to get up with the alarm clock, and not hit the snooze button, meant that I got to enjoy the peace and tranquility of the early morning -- without interruptions, phone calls, messages, traffic noise, and air pollution.

I highly recommend getting up an hour before you think you need to, and simply relishing that early-morning simplicity and freshness. Put on some smooth music and get a head start on the day by being calm, before the busyness starts.

Changing my eating and drinking habits was next. As a bachelor, I was a lazy food shopper and a lazy eater. In some ways, this worked in my favor, as I rarely had extra food in the house, so I didn't overeat! But I did need to lose some weight and eat healthier food. I'd forgotten about the importance of fruits and vegetables, and started to eat both regularly. Regarding drinks, I did allow myself a beer after work, but I noticed that I drank beer while watching TV as more of a tactile habit – it wasn't the beer, rather it was having something to drink. I substituted club soda, and saw the results quickly: I was not dehydrated at all in the mornings, and was more clear-headed. On top of that, it was also cheaper! Soon, I didn't even want that daily beer, and restricted beer drinking to weekends.

I now had a platform on which I could start improving my life. And I didn't miss the extra hours of TV or additional beers. I actually felt better without them. With the extra time, energy, and money, I was able to acquire books about how to make myself a better person. I still gave myself time to unwind – we are not machines, and everyone needs to rest and laugh. But I cut the TV time down to an hour, and then was able to accept a part-time editing job. I would never have accepted such a job when I was on my previous nightly "schedule."

Importantly, I would get into bed before I was sleepy, which enabled me to read a self-improving book about business or how to be more motivated. As Jim Rohn has said, "If you want to be wealthy, study wealth," and there is an abundance of books on this topic out there waiting for you. The quote that helps sum it all up is one from Ben Franklin, and one that many of us heard in our youth: "Early to bed, and early to rise, makes a man healthy, wealthy, and wise."

LIFE AND CHANGE

Life doesn't like it when we refuse to change. It basically says to us, "If you expect *me* to

> *Life doesn't like it when we refuse to change.*

change, I expect *you* to change too." The problem is that for the depressive, who is also a pessimist, change is always seen as going from bad to worse. We have a mentality of "Better the devil you know, than the devil you don't," and actually start to feel safe in our tunnel of unhappiness, because we think we have control. In fact, we don't. And when change inevitably comes from the outside, we react with surprise and anger, refusing to accept that you can only "escape" change for a very short amount of time.

As I mentioned at the beginning of this book, at 20 I was happy-go-lucky and by my early 30s I was in the doldrums of depression. What changed? To begin, everything had changed except *me*. In my early 30s, I was still trying to live with the perspective of a 20-year-old: that life should be 100% fun and that there were no repercussions to a lifestyle of complete hedonism. Work, for me, was a "job," with no concept of a *career* – and this non-productive mentality soon catches up with you.

Here are some changes we can start making today:

> *Many people take better care of their cars than of their own bodies.*

- Diet: It's amazing how many people take better care of their cars than of their own bodies. Put the best "oil" into your own engine. Eat vegetables, fruit, lean meat; drink plenty of water (the hotter the better), and cut down on the desserts.

- Sleeping schedule: as mentioned, get into bed before you are sleepy, with a book that teaches you something.

- Scene: Aside from work, where do you spend your time? If you are mostly at home, take a close look at what you see there every day. We become so accustomed to our homes that we forget what they look like inside, and hence how they are affecting us. During the most stressful time of my life, when I had far too much going on in my head, I also had a cluttered apartment. Organizing my possessions – and throwing quite a few of them away – gave me a nice, clean, spacious-looking apartment to come home to every night. Likewise, when you are feeling depressed and that life is dull, put some decorations on the walls, such as posters of your favorite band. It's amazing how powerful the subconscious can be in influencing your mood.

- Appearance: most people have their own style, but one should dress in a manner that accentuates his or her best features, and looks presentable. You can't completely control the way you were born, but you can control how you dress. There's not many things in life that we can control, but what we wear is one of them.

- Learning more. Ask yourself: When was the last time I learned something new? Not facts from the news, but a new skill or ability?

- Perspective: you've already taken the first step in changing that. Keep reading.

These are relatively large-scale changes, and after making them, you can focus on the smaller ones. At one point, the items on my list of things to change included drinking less alcohol, being less sarcastic, and reading more books about personal finance.

On External Change

> *God can grant you many things, but not external stability.*

A quick note on external change. God can grant you many things: strength in adversity, understanding, patience, perhaps even seeing opportunities. What he cannot give you is external stability. Change is as inherent in life as breathing, and perhaps even more so. To refuse to change is to bang your head against a brick wall.

I'm not asking you to like it. At least not immediately. But if something is a fact, we have no choice but to accept it. An excellent parable on dealing with external change is found in Spencer Johnson's *Who Moved My Cheese*. You can read it in an hour, and it is told in the familiar style of a fable. It teaches us how to see opportunity in change, and how the sooner we accept change, the faster we can move forward with our lives.

2 NEGATIVITY

For many years I was known as "Mr. Negative." Regardless of how positive something was, I found a reason to complain. Most likely, I would have found something to dislike in Paradise. Ironically, the only person who didn't notice this was me. In my view, I was seeing the world as it really was: there was something wrong with everything, and that "something" was what I focused on.

I woke up each day despising myself and my life. My perspective on life, at the time, could be summed up as "Everything sucks." Does this sound familiar?

Negativity is a broad concept, but it is actually very simple: it is a mode of thinking. Negativity is both a product and symptom of "tunnel vision," and will precipitate you into a spiral of disliking your life and wishing the world would end.

TUNNEL VISION

The concept of Tunnel Vision will be discussed throughout this book. For now, it refers to a limited perspective that is a result of anxiety, depression, and negativity. As with being in a tunnel, it limits the way we see ourselves, our lives, and the world around us, forcing us to only see it through the negativity in our minds.

One of the worst parts of being in a State of Negativity is one's contempt for the positive. I talk more about this in my chapter on Developing Happiness, but for now, the dangers of negativity are twofold: the ignorance of how to see positivity, and the lack of respect for optimistic viewpoints on life.

AVOIDING COMPARISONS

Making comparisons is natural to human nature. Somewhere in our DNA, there is something that compels us to compare ourselves to those around us. Likewise, there is an inborn tendency to evaluate everything in relation to something else. And hence we have the phrase, "The grass is always greener on the other side of the fence."

Making comparisons puts you on the fast track to feeling bad about yourself.

If one chooses the habit of comparing everything, then the grass on the other side of the fence will always be greener. This is something you must accept. You need to look at what gives you peace of mind and a foundation for happiness: financial security, maintaining your health, spare time for recreation, etc., without the constant need to look around you. Making comparisons puts you on the fast track to feeling bad about yourself.

For several years, I constantly had my financial situation hanging over all of my thoughts. It was like a curtain, blocking out the sunlight of my life. I had friends, my health, a nice social life, hobbies – and all was shrouded by my constant thinking about how I was poorer than everyone else. Bear in mind, I wasn't starving, and I had a disposable income. It was just that I was obsessed about not being financially where I should have been, and not being at the same level as others.

One Friday morning, as I was looking at a smooth day at work and then a weekend full of dinners and a sunny barbecue with friends, I realized that I wasn't really looking forward to any of these pleasures. In the back of my mind, or more appropriately, in the front, I knew wasn't going to enjoy them, as I was going to be constantly dwelling on my money "problems."

I took a look at myself, and said that I could not keep going on like this. Perhaps my financial situation would improve, but not immediately, and perhaps not for several years. Was I going to live the rest of my life like this – not enjoying anything, with my mind constantly elsewhere?

It didn't seem wise, and it definitely didn't seem *fun*. Sure, it was important to care about money, but it wasn't helpful to obsess about it. And I told my mind that I wasn't going to stand for it. The mind had to stop painting over the happy moments of my life with the veneer of financial stress. The people I was meeting didn't care if I was poorer than they were, and most of them didn't even know my money situation. To go on like this meant, quite simply, not enjoying life at all for quite a long period of time.

Pyrrhic Victories

I also thought about how I would feel if I stressed for a few years and then made the money I wanted. What would I look back on? It reminded me of the person I was in high school – an ambitious student who stopped at nothing to achieve the highest marks, and who made himself and everyone around him miserable. Ultimately I got the grades I wanted, but it was a "Pyrrhic victory."

This term is useful to know, as it originates from the world of battle and is applicable in regular life. Just a bit of background: in 279 BC, the Greek general Pyrrhus (pronounced *PEER-us*) invaded the Romans in southern Italy. The two armies engaged in the fierce Battle of Asculum. While Pyrrhus' army technically won, he lost so many soldiers, including many officers, that his fighting force was significantly weakened for future engagements in the campaign. Shortly after the battle, he said, "If we are victorious in one more battle with the Romans, we shall be utterly ruined." Hence, the term "Pyrrhic victory" signifies a victory won at too great a cost.

This concept of a Pyrrhic victory is one which arises when we have a desire which makes us miserable in the process of achieving it. Hard work in pursuit of a goal is certainly admirable. But when the pursuit of that goal becomes deeply unpleasant, when you are disliking every day of your life and bringing unhappiness to those around you, the final attainment of that goal will be a Pyrrhic victory. If you are not enjoying the journey at all, you will have ruined yourself by the time you reach the destination.

"I hope the world ends"

My negativity, which led to hopelessness, gave rise to wishing that the world would end. This, I believed, would release me from any obligations to enjoy life or to be successful. In a sense, it was a suicidal wish – the wish to die and be rid of this "horrible" world.

> *There's no point in wishing for the world to end.*

To those of you who suffer from this kind of thinking, I have news for you: the world is not going to end anytime soon. Whoever has designed this world in which we live is not going to sit by and watch it go up in a puff of smoke. Right now, that may seem like bad news, but by the end of this book, you will see why that news is very good.

In order to start becoming a less negative person, it is essential to understand that negativity is a *choice*. It is not an immutable condition, it is not forced on you, and it is not in any way productive. Yes, certain circumstances are negative, and yes, some things in life just *suck*. Losing a child, for example, is a cloud without a silver lining. But here we are talking about a mentality. I am reminded of a quote from the ancient Greek philosopher Epictetus, that "Men are disturbed not by things, but by the view which they take of them." This is echoed by a line in the Talmud: "We do not see things as they are. We see things as *we* are."

Switching Perspectives

The quotes above reinforce the fact that most of our problems are problems of perception. It is amazing how deeply this affects our daily life. In my case, I used to dislike being asked "How's work?" because in my view, I always focused on the negative. For me, every day was a "bad day." All I focused on was the sale I hadn't made, the client who was annoying, the bad traffic on the way to the meeting.

When I put myself on the path to positivity, "How's work?" became a question that I started to enjoy answering. Yes, there were "bad days," but the vast majority were good. I focused on the positive aspects of the day: rather than the one annoying phone call, I thought about the good calls and meetings that I had. I saw my attitude towards work improve as a result, as well as my performance level.

Part of switching your perspective involves changing your vocabulary.

Part of switching your perspective involves changing your vocabulary. We often don't realize the impact of the words that we use every day, even when talking to ourselves. I used to be a person who said he "hated" many things, and the result was that it made me more negative. "Hate" is a strong word, and carries with it a very negative passion. Part of redirecting my energy to being positive, along with assuming an attitude of gratitude, was removing the word "hate" from my wordbank.

The beginning of a positive perspective involves being thankful for the good things in your life. If you can read, you have something to be thankful for. The same goes for having daily meals, having eyes to see and ears to hear with, being able to walk, having family and friends, and the other positive aspects of our lives which we commonly take for granted. We don't take negative things for granted, so why should we do so with positive ones?

Another factor in becoming more positive was changing my attitude towards details. I had always thought that "The devil is in the details," i.e. that the more closely you had to look at something, the worse it became. This was especially the case when I was in sales and was dealing with contracts. Details represented the inevitable stumbling block.

Nonetheless, one must accept that details are a part of life. They are always there, and to dislike them

Fear of details is a sign of negativity.

is to go against nature. Learn that details can be a good thing. Fear of details is a sign of negativity. Would you want to have a surgeon who didn't like details? Or a financial advisor? Let yourself gracefully accept them, and face them as a challenge that can be overcome.

As I became a happier person, I also started to hear myself complain. I hadn't realized it, but complaining had become my main form of conversation. It was a miracle that I still had friends, but a good friend is a miracle in itself. The more I heard myself complain, the more I got sick of it, and made a conscious effort to stop.

Nevertheless, we are all human. Sometimes you are just going to have a day where you are grumpy. Give yourself permission to feel like this. But also recognize that it is *you* who is feeling this way, not others, and that you owe it to yourself to get out of this state and to not take out your frustrations on other people. In short, don't be too hard on yourself, and keep the feelings of others in mind.

3   CONTROL AND FOCUS

Happiness and peace of mind begin with a clear understanding of one principle: A few things are within your control. And nearly all things are not. One of our challenges to living a happy life is learning to accept this simple fact.

Taken from a distant perspective, the world is not an easy environment in which to live. The Darwinian notion of survival is indeed a fact of life. In the US at least, we are entering a period in which the middle class is not growing, and in which the prosperity which we took for granted has now become a big question mark. Each day, we are beset by conflicts, over which our control is often limited. We cannot control the actions of other human beings, or the weather, or large-scale things like the economy or the job market.

With television and the Internet, the world around us is also constantly encouraging us to take an interest in other people's "business." In some ways this is a good thing, as we can see who is in need of our help. But overall, it is something to be wary of, as we start to compare ourselves to others and take too much interest in other people's lives.

SETTING YOUR SCOPE

At the onset of my descent into unhappiness, seeing those around me become more successful -- while I stagnated -- was not something that I should have thought about constantly, and it definitely didn't help my depression.

> *Focus on the things that you CAN control.*

What *did* help, was putting a fence around my concerns and telling myself that things outside of my influence were not something I should be thinking about. I have always learned things the hard way -- something I hope to help you avoid by reading this book – and I had to teach myself a phrase I keep in mind every day: Focus on the things that you *can* control. As much as it would be nice to force everything to go as you wished, this is not something that you can do. And if you have an appreciation for other people's happiness – a characteristic of any happy person – you don't want to prioritize your happiness over theirs.

One lecture that we often give children is, "The world does not revolve around you." Nonetheless, how often do we get frustrated because we expect exactly that? When we become upset or angry that things aren't going as we wanted, or planned, we are essentially saying, "I want the world to revolve around *me*!" Well, of course you do! Who wouldn't? But if the world revolved around each individual, we'd be in chaos. Which is why it does not revolve around any one person. It is one of those things which is fair to all but which isn't really "great" for anyone.

Let's look at a short list of the things that you *can* control:

- Your learning: You can learn and gain knowledge

- Your general health: You can eat right, drink water, do exercise. None of these take too much time or are expensive. (As I have proven to myself over the years, you don't need to join a gym in order to exercise.)

- Helping others: If you live in a city, there are plenty of poor people within reach. If you live in the suburbs or countryside, there are charity organizations to join.

- Your positivity level: In addition to this book, there are other volumes about how to be positive.

- Your punctuality at work, and overall reliability and efficiency

- Lastly, you can control your perspective on calmness, i.e. making calmness and composure your first priority in all situations. Focus on making it your "go-to" feeling. This won't be natural at first, but in time, equanimity will develop into a habit and will become automatic.

THE GOAL OF HAVING GOALS

This is not a book about professional success, but there is a definite overlap, in the goals department, between success and happiness. Human nature likes to *achieve*. And to achieve – whether success, happiness, or peace of mind – we need to focus.

Focus is an essential part of having peace of mind.

Focus is an essential part of having peace of mind. We often think of peace of mind as being a dreamy, hazy state, whereas actually it is a state of being focused. The inability to focus is related to overthinking and anxiety. With overthinking, your mind is tossed into the wind; with anxiety, your mind feels the need to jump from one negative topic to another.

In order to focus, we need goals. In fact, it is impossible to discuss the importance of focus without discussing goals and how crucial they are to having a stable and happy life.

Most of us have heard goals mentioned since we were young and in school. However, school makes goals easy to define. The academic establishment gives us the short-term goals of passing tests, and the long-term goals of getting into good colleges. (This unfortunately continues into college, where we are more concerned – and consumed – with passing exams than with finding a career that suits us.)

Regardless of school, once we are out and on our own, goals become more significant and essential: they help us to *achieve*, but just as important, they keep the mind composed and disciplined. The mind likes to have a focus. It can do its best work, and reach its maximum potential, when it is not spreading itself across too many areas.

One unfortunate aspect of adult life, as hinted above, is that life does not define our goals for us – and we are busy with work, family, and errands. If pressed as to what their goals are, many people would simply say "To get through the week" or "To not be bothered by my boss." Such goals are certainly not very motivating, and in some ways they are very negative.

For many years of my life, I had no goals except getting to Friday night so I could enjoy the weekend. The years passed by, and when I paused and took a look at my life, I realized that aside from a small promotion, I'd accomplished very little. No real financial savings, no challenge that I'd overcome. In high school I had wanted to know everything that could be known, to bench-press 350 pounds, to accomplish other feats. What had happened to these goals? It will also come as no surprise that I had lost all of my psychological footing: with a mind continually overthinking and running wild, and a character with no ambition, I was someone who had become pessimistic and very depressed.

I deceived myself by saying that I had chosen to only "enjoy" my life, and that I didn't need goals. In fact, I had stopped enjoying it. My life had become empty, and instead of having a clear aim, it was full of unnecessary little complications.

Having goals provides you with the simplicity that leads you to peace of mind. A life without goals is a messy and complicated one, because there is no focus. In its lack of simplicity, it is aimless and painful.

> *A life without goals is a messy and complicated one.*

21

SETTING GOALS

So how do we go about setting goals for ourselves? It begins by thinking of what gives us a foundation to be happy. The words "health" and "money" should immediately come to mind. Yes, money isn't everything, but we sure need it to live. If money is a concern in your life -- and for most of us it is -- then one of your goals is to make more of it.

This is unfortunately one of the hardest things to do, and there are plenty of books that will help you draw a map. However, once you start acknowledging the importance of your economic future, you can think of strategies to get there. What has worked in my case, has been setting a savings goal for each year. I only started this in my 30s, but I wish I'd started earlier. Bear in mind that this would only be a short-term goal. A long-term goal would involve how to use that money as an investment.

Nonetheless, not all goals are financial. One of my friends has the hobby of running marathons every few months – a short-term goal which also has a great benefit to his health. He is able to focus on making sure he is physically fit to run that grueling race; and when he does run it and finish it, he receives the feeling of happiness which one only gets from *accomplishment.*

A good goal involves enjoying both the journey and the destination.

A good goal is one that brings you some measure of enjoyment while you are pursuing it. Hence, a good goal involves enjoying both the journey and the destination.

SIMPLICITY

One of the many helpful observations of Marcus Aurelius is that "Very little indeed is necessary for living

Simplifying does not mean achieving less.

a happy life." Simplicity plays an enormous role in achieving peace of mind. We spend a lot of time and energy clogging up our heads with things that we cannot control and which, in the end, don't matter. Simplifying does not mean achieving less. Ultimately, it means achieving *more*. By keeping our wants under control, we actually focus on the wants that are most important to us, and this builds momentum.

It is not wrong to want more than you have, as long as that "want" is something healthy and helpful. The opposite of a healthy want is *addiction*, the state in which one's fondness for something (or someone) becomes self-destructive. It can be in the form of drugs, alcohol, work, sex, and even such apparently benign things as exercise. It can also involve an uncontrolled passion for material things and keeping up with your neighbors.

Some people go into a foul mood for days when their favorite sports team loses; others get emotional over political issues, get in arguments, and ruin their day. Such distractions destroy our ability to focus on things that will make our lives better, and then add to the whirlwind of thoughts going through our heads. I'm not saying that we should have no concerns other than our own goals, but I do say that our goals themselves need to take priority. You can't help others if you haven't helped yourself. Realize your objective and get on the path, and then you have a foundation.

FOCUS AND ANXIETY

When you find your anxiety acting up, focus on your goals instead. Think about how great it will be to make that sale, buy that house, finish that project. Channel your overthinking into your goals and aspirations.

I once had a choice to spend two days in "limbo," a state of stress and uncertainty, when a good client sent me an email saying that he was disappointed with a recent project, adding that he would discuss it with me "after the weekend." I thought this was unfair, but there was nothing I could do to get the answer from him earlier. After an hour of worrying about what the client would eventually say, I realized that the worrying wasn't going to go away on its own. Anxiety is in my nature. Instead, I could focus on something that would actually be productive. All that mental energy could either be focused on accomplishing something, or on worrying about something that I could not change.

One of my close friends has always said that it is useless to worry about anything for more than an hour. That amount of time, he feels, is sufficient for the human mind – which operates at speeds of a fraction of a second – to go over whatever the source is of the worrying (probably several times) and reach whatever conclusions it is going to reach. After that hour, you're just rehashing stuff that you've already given plenty of attention to.

I kept this in mind when dealing with my client. While I had already spent an hour on the train pondering this, I took out a pen and paper and made a list of the things he could be annoyed about. We were working on three projects, and since there was nothing else, he had to be annoyed about something involving these. I made a few bullet-points for each, and then I was done. Whatever he could be annoyed about had to be within those points. And then I closed my notebook and my mind was free to think about other things.

My friend's advice leads to the ideal state of being able to control one's focus, that of being able to "compartmentalize." This ability is seen in high-level operators such as politicians and CEOs, and of course in surgeons, who have to block out any causes of unpleasantness and distraction when handling very sensitive situations. It becomes more achievable as we reach a greater state of peace of mind as well as more confidence in being able to handle difficulties; the less confidence we have, the more we are inclined to stress over a task, and to either try to finish it abruptly or procrastinate while letting it fester in our conscious mind. Please note that compartmentalizing is not multitasking. The latter is an attempt to handle multiple things simultaneously; compartmentalizing means putting them in the right mental place for the appropriate time.

The first step in learning how to compartmentalize, is to become confident that you will be able to do the task -- and this confidence comes from positivity. If you are not confident, you will worry, and you will think that worrying will help. But if you are positive, you will be confident that you can put the matter to the side for a short period of time, and then come back to it and deal with it successfully.

DEALING WITH STRESS

Stress has always been a part of human existence. It is not a new concept. If we look at human history, there has always been the stress of having unlimited wants and limited resources. There has always been the demand to eat, to be warm and clothed, and to feel fulfilled. So what has changed? Why do we now see stress levels that are off the charts?

The cynical answer is that people have become less capable of handling stress. We live in a world where gratification is only seconds away, and in which there are numerous alternatives to work. It is a world which provides many opportunities for fun. Hence, some will say that our threshold for stress is very low -- that we pamper ourselves and expect to be pampered. The stress of everyday life thus seems amplified as a result.

I find this view cynical, because I happen to like the world that we live in. Of course it is not perfect, just as the world 10,000 years ago wasn't perfect. It is not our "fault" that gratification is only seconds away; we work hard and want to be rewarded. At the same time, there are aspects of the modern world that are responsible for stress levels. The world of knowledge, and the mind, has increased dramatically over the millennia. The human body has not. While we are overall taller and live longer, the body itself has not evolved at the same pace as the mind. Humans used to walk several miles a day, lift heavy amounts from dawn to dusk, and then sleep. Nowadays, we get through the day with very little physical exercise required at all. We go to work by car or train, we sit for nine hours or more at a computer, go home again by car or train, and then sit down on chairs or sofas until we lie down to sleep.

Simply put, we biologically are not matching the levels of activity going on in our minds. On top of this, we have text messages, emails, Facebook, Skype, Whatsapp, constant interruptions, and a world that demands more from us each day professionally. I've had several jobs working in cities, in which my commute to work was a brisk 20-minute walk, and I always found that I started the workday with less anxiety. I'd burned it off. Likewise, the 20-minute walk home at the end of the day helped me to get rid of the day's pressures, and made my evenings much more pleasant. A walk in the middle of the afternoon, if it had been possible, would have done wonders. One would think that employers would encourage their staff to go out for a walk at lunchtime or to even schedule a "walking session" for the entire team at some point during each workday.

Having learned more about control, I still have my occasional problems with focus, though they appear on a small scale. These often appear less as problems but more as "challenges," which is the way that a positive person should view problems. They are often trivial. One day, after work, I could not find a certain black shirt I wanted to wear, and began looking for it frenetically. I said to myself, "I don't lose things. How could I lose it? Where could it possibly have gone?" I was faced with two roads: calming down, or catastrophizing the situation into thinking that I was becoming chronically forgetful. The latter was the way I had lived my life for many years: turning everything into a catastrophe. In the midst of this, I said to myself, "Can I control the way I am acting? Can I put this out of my mind till tomorrow, when I can call the laundromat and ask them if they found a black shirt?" It was a test – a challenge, to see if I could control my anxiety. What I found out, was that I could. I forbade myself to keep thinking about it, and after a few minutes, I didn't have it on my mind anymore.

This is of course a simple example. Worrying about a job or a loved one's health – or indeed your own – is much more serious than worrying about the whereabouts of a shirt. However, what I was able to confirm from this experience is that anxiety is not an all-powerful force, and that if I can control it for small things, I can eventually control it for the big ones.

Before we go further, start listing the things that you *can* control, and after that, make a list of the things that you cannot. This list will help you to establish perspective.

4 ANXIETY

Anxiety influences our thoughts and ultimately our way of acting. It is one of the most powerful forces that we cannot see.

I mentioned anxiety in the first chapter, and indeed, anxiety has been my most formidable obstacle to happiness. For most of my life, I never identified this as a problem, perhaps because there was not as much widespread awareness of anxiety as there is now, and also because of the tendency for it to be simply explained as "excessive worrying." Worrying tends to be associated with a present problem, whereas anxiety is a long-term issue and ultimately a condition.

Anxiety has been a constant companion of mine, for as long as I can remember. My experience with anxiety began at a young age, though I didn't realize what it was at the time. I started to feel moderate anxiety pangs even in late elementary school. Any type of long-term "project" assigned by my teachers filled me with nervousness that I would never get it done, that I would get overwhelmed, and that I would not get a high grade.

PERSONAL EXPERIENCES

The earliest experience that comes to mind is 5th Grade (11 years old), when my classmates and I were each asked to do a report on one of the US states. I recall the teacher trying to console me by saying that the project wasn't as formidable as my mind was making it out to be; I also recall tormenting my parents by complaining and stressing.

By 6th grade, the next year, I was worse. In one instance, I was assigned a book report and complained about it all through the school day, to the point that my best friend told me I was "being stupid." It wasn't stupidity, but it was my anxiety taking over. In my high school years, I was a very difficult person to be around, for both my family and my teachers, due to my anxiety over achieving academic perfection.

Anxiety is a master of deception. In time, my inability to handle anxiety – and failure to recognize it as a condition that transformed my way of thinking and acting -- led to me avoiding situations or courses with long-term requirements. It led to the fear, and the dislike, of any task that had more than just a few steps. And in life, the things that require more than a few steps tend to be the ones that are the most important and worthwhile.

I mention my early experience as it illustrates that anxiety is not something that suddenly befalls us, but something that we are either born with or which appears in us at a very young age. It is certainly not a choice, nor is it something that we can see coming.

ANXIETY'S UNFORTUNATE POWER

The difference between anxiety and general worrying is that anxiety is both physical and chemical, in addition to being psychological. Self-help guru Dale Carnegie, famous for his book *How to Win Friends and Influence People*, addresses the concept of worry in *How to Stop Worrying and Start Living*. The book contains strategies that are helpful, though it treats worrying as more of a "habit" than a condition. Carnegie suggests always saying to yourself, "What's the worst that can happen?", though for the anxiety sufferer, thinking about the worst – thinking negatively – will ultimately be destructive. Anxiety, fused with negativity, is a deadly mixture, and will kill your peace of mind and your happiness.

Unfortunately, anxiety and negativity feed off of each other. Every chapter of this book reinforces positive thinking, and as you become less negative, you will find your anxiety abating as well. Keep in mind that anxiety is harder to overcome, as it is a chemical condition, whereas negativity is a choice.

> *Anxiety and negativity feed off of each other.*

Anxiety is a "proactive" phenomenon. That does not mean that it is "positive." Rather, what I mean by "proactive" in this sense is that the mind searches for something to worry about, and feels uncomfortable when it does not have an object of stress. You are eventually imprisoned in this way of thinking, and worry that something bad will happen if you *stop* worrying. Anxiety confines you, with several layers, and creates a cycle for itself to live on.

Anxiety makes the attainment of long-term goals nearly impossible, and renders the anxiety victim unlikely to even *have* long-term objectives. However, long-term goals are essential to a feeling of fulfillment and to having a degree of success, whether financial or otherwise. Take a look at yourself and see if you have any pursuits, professional or recreational, that are of a long-term nature. In the depths of my anxiety, I tended to choose hobbies which were unquantifiable and which were not goal-oriented, such as reading – something I could do completely at my own pace, by myself, which did not take very long, and in which there was no emphasis on reaching a certain level.

What to Do

For the anxiety sufferer, a long-term goal should be seen as the sum of several short-term goals, with each clearly defined. It should not be seen as a separate entity. A daily focus that is exclusively on the long-term, without breaking it down into parts, will not allow your mind to rest; it will make you worry, make you second-guess having it, make you think too much, and finally lower your happiness level and increase your depression. You don't want too much time to think about something. While it is good to be on a path, make your milestones related to each other, and cumulative. Hence, break your goals down into units with which you are comfortable.

> *Much of anxiety is really a fear of the unknown.*

Much of anxiety is really a fear of the unknown. We might know that we have to give a presentation or take a test the next day, but we don't know how it will go. The "unknown" is not just something grand and mysterious, like life after death. It can be getting a request from a colleague or client and not understanding or knowing what do to. And it is difficult to prepare for the unknown. So what to do?

The only thing you can do is to receive the unknown and act with recognition and equanimity. This means allowing yourself to be surprised but to quickly shift to a mode of breaking the situation down into parts and seeing how each one can be solved.

Along with this equanimity is the acceptance that anxiety will always be part of your life, to some degree. I believe

Carefully managed, anxiety can still be part of a smooth and happy life.

that a tendency towards anxiety is inborn: it is just a question of how you recognize it and control it. As a companion, it gives you the sense to avoid taking harmful risks – the self-responsibility to assess risks carefully. Carefully managed, it can still be part of a smooth and happy life, as long as you are quick to acknowledge when it is consuming your thinking.

What we need to say to ourselves, when we are feeling the world closing in on us, and barely able to function, is that that we are

With an anxiety attack, we are operating with Tunnel Vision.

in The Tunnel. With an anxiety attack, we are operating with Tunnel Vision. As this tunnel prevents us from seeing the light of reason, rational arguments are not going to be effective against it. It is a time when we need to be in motion – and unfortunately, the weight of an anxiety attack can be paralyzing, partly because it makes our mind think negatively about everything.

With an anxiety attack, one's energy should be used to be physically active. Running, walking, pushups – anything cardiovascular that focuses your mind on the exercise itself. Passive things, like reading, will not be effective. The mind has to be forced to *stop thinking*. Make sure that the motion is continuous. Weight training, which involves sets of several repetitions, punctuated by lengthy periods between sets, is not effective, as it allows too much time for thinking. While resting between sets, your mind goes back into Overthinking mode. No – to fight this, you need to limit the amount of time for the mind to get into this state.

CHEMICAL AVOIDANCE

I get much fewer anxiety attacks than I did in the past, though as mentioned, anxiety is a "companion" and will probably never disappear from my life completely. In my experience, the mornings were always the worst. I would wake up thinking of my failures, my mistakes, and my precarious financial situation. One thing I discovered was that drinking alcohol the night before, especially excessive amounts, led to hangovers where the anxiety attacks were more severe. A similar phenomenon would happen after a week of heavy alcohol consumption, in which I would experience "DT," i.e. the shaking that results from withdrawal from alcohol. I would then experience onslaughts of panic and anxiety.

As with many things in life, the solution was simple and required me to simplify: drink less alcohol. On top of that – and this was critical – I avoided drinking caffeine the next morning, and altogether. Stimulants are very detrimental to the serenity of an anxiety-sufferer, and caffeine is one of the worst. It unfortunately took me some time to see how seriously my anxiety levels were aggravated by tea and coffee. The latter affects me so unfavorably that I cannot drink it at all. It is not a major issue – I can still enjoy the smell of it, and for those who crave the taste, there is decaf. If you find that you do need caffeine, drink some weak tea.

Below are some practical ways to handle anxiety:

- Keep yourself well-fed. A steady, regular intake of food keeps your body strong for dealing with the mental stress that anxiety causes.

- Exercise: Related to eating, exercise keeps you physically strong, while also serving as a channel through which to shed the burden of anxiety.

- Music and humor: I discuss these in a later chapter, but for now, they both serve as ways of diverting the mind and keeping it occupied with positivity.

- Be around positive people.

- Avoid chemical stimulants, especially caffeine.

- If you cannot avoid worrying, designate a specific time each week to focus on what bothers you (e.g. your money situation). You will find that you approach the worrying in a more structured fashion, of seeing how to fix the problem rather than just worry about it.

- Learn to break things down into parts.

- When you are intensely worried about something, tell yourself that you will do it in the best manner possible.

Using these tactics will reduce both the frequency and intensity of anxiety attacks. You will also have greater awareness of when these attacks are coming, and will be able to fight them off.

5 DEPRESSION

Whereas anxiety can be likened to a "throbbing" sort of pain, depression is a "dull" pain,

> *Depression is a mode, not just a mood.*

metaphorically like carrying around a load of heavy weight that puts strain on your bones. I use the word "depressed" to denote a *mode*, not a just mood. We may informally describe someone as "depressed" when his favorite sports team loses a championship, or when he hears some bad news from a client. However, being in a *state* of depression unfortunately becomes a way of life -- one that is chronic and blinding.

Much has been written on why people are depressed – much more than about why they are happy. Like anxiety, depression is a state of tunnel vision, and unfortunately of facing the darkness rather than the light. It is a state of mental and emotional exhaustion, of negativity, and of limited perspective. I experienced a serious depression, and can certainly say that at its core was a deep feeling of negativity, which we call Hopelessness.

The depressive is also a victim of deception. As with myself, I didn't realize I was actually *in* a depression. My perception of reality had totally skewed towards the negative, but in my mind, I thought I was viewing everything objectively.

VICTIMS OF DEPRESSION

Depression was an eye-opener, as it made me able to understand others who suffered from the same condition. There is a point in one's descent into depression where logic and reason are left behind, and where we convince ourselves that everything is negative. It can happen to people of all descriptions, though one cardinal rule is that the more inclined you are to overthink, the more likely you are to be depressed.

Otherwise, depression does not discriminate. The classic example involves depression affecting the wealthy. For many years, I found it incomprehensible that rich people could have depression problems. To me, who had battled financial difficulties, it didn't make sense that people with financial freedom had anything to be unhappy about. Simply put, a life without money problems seemed a life without *any* problems. Or so I thought. Rich people can actually fall into a depression, obviously not for financial reasons, but as a result of a wide range of things, nearly all of which are shared by people from less wealthy circumstances. Aside from money, there are plenty of other problems that anyone can have – family, health, a lack of spiritual fulfillment, etc.

Related to that, depression can be initiated by failure and a misunderstanding of failure's place in our lives. An overreaction to failure can cause a sharp descent downwards, especially if it is combined with or catalyzed by having a negative way of thinking. At the same time, an accumulated feeling that one has not fulfilled herself can also initiate that dangerous downward slide.

As I will often say in this book, the more reflective one gets, the more inclined he or she is to be *For the depressive, the past is the enemy.* depressed. And unfortunately, when we are depressed we think about our past – all of our mistakes, failures, and missed opportunities. It is tempting to want to think about the past and to see where we went wrong. But bear in mind that if you are suffering from depression, the past is dangerous. All memories, even happy ones, become tainted with the stain of negativity. For the depressive, the past is the enemy. You will quickly focus on the unpleasant parts of those memories, and will amplify them. I discuss the past more thoroughly in a later chapter.

COMBATING AND ASCENDING

The mind of a depressive is angled in such a way as to focus on the negative. As I have said above, depression is a mode, not just a mood. It is a state which colors your perspective on everything around you. In my case, I descended into a stage of depression in which I didn't even realize that I was depressed. Thinking negatively had become a way of life.

I am a firm believer that we don't reach happiness alone – if I didn't feel this way, there would be no point in this book – and in both *The ascent out of depression begins with recognition.*

cases of my depression, I was able to rise out of it with some help from others. However, I had also already recognized that I was in a depressed state, and had started to remedy it as best I could. The ascent out of depression begins with recognition.

As my depression was generated by frustration with my career, it was professional opportunities that finally helped me escape; but I would never have received, or even seen, these opportunities if I hadn't started to lift myself out of the depression hole on my own.

My first active step to getting better was to stop saying that my life "sucked," and to admit to myself that there were indeed some positive things in my life. I had a very kind family, nice friends, and my physical health. There were other positive things, but these really stood out. I didn't go down the path of comparing myself to people who lack these things, as making comparisons doesn't help you to feel better, but I did keep in mind that there are plenty of people who struggle just to attain these core requirements for happiness. In short, I started to put myself into what Life Coaches call an "attitude of gratitude."

Once this attitude starts, it gains momentum, and you find yourself appreciating more and more things about your life. I started realizing how grateful I was for music, for blue skies, for the sounds of ocean waves, for laughter. Simple things. I realized that although there were some aspects of my life that were not particularly good, especially my job at the time, there were many other aspects that were very positive.

I brought myself back to thinking more realistically, with a balanced perspective. This enabled me to take an optimistic view of applying for new jobs, or even talking about new opportunities. In my state of depression, I hadn't had a positive view of opportunities; after rejecting the ones that I had, new ones had stopped coming to me.

As mentioned, I didn't get out of my career doldrums alone. But I would never have even gone to the job interviews, let alone passed them, if I hadn't started to change my perspective.

Perspective is not the only dimension of depression. I fully recognize that depression is a monumental, paralyzing force that comes like a thief in the night. Depression is a state where the mind has exhausted its natural reservoir of positivity – and we are all born with different levels. Indeed, there are people born with high happiness levels, for whom it is actually very difficult to become depressed. If you know one of these people, keep them close.

Tips for fighting depression:

- First, identify that you are in a state of depression. If you have already done so, then congratulate yourself. It means you are on your way out of the tunnel.

- Write down the positive things about your life. This is critically important.

- Avoid depressing TV shows and music

- Keep yourself in motion. Go for brisk walks of 30 minutes. Exercise is not easy for the depressive. He or she is too bogged down with negative thoughts to want to improve the body and thereby prolong existence. Thus, don't make an elaborate exercise plan – you will quickly see it as a burden, and will stop doing it. The quick walks are cheap and can be done anytime.

- Foods that can help: I do not put a huge amount of faith in the effects of food on one's mental state. To me, this is almost equivalent to equating food with a drug. Nonetheless, eating a diet that is healthy, full of vegetables, will help you to have energy and to avoid being ill, both of which are cornerstones of being a happier person.

- Alcohol is just a short-term "solution". In no way will alcohol, or narcotics, take you out of depression.

- Avoid long periods of solitude. True, it may be difficult to motivate yourself to be around people, but muster up your energy and go see them.

- Accept that you are not "sinning" by not being happy. We are required to obey the laws, but being unhappy is not illegal. At the same time, start taking action.

Lastly, fix the things that can be fixed. If it's your weight, start eating better and doing some exercise. If your home is a mess, clean it up. If you've had an argument with a friend, apologize and get past it. Fix the easy things, and you'll gain confidence about the harder things.

If it is not distinct as to what is making you depressed, take a look at all of the possibilities. If you still cannot figure out what is making you unhappy, you need to start redefining your understanding of happiness. The mind can continuously learn, and can continuously adapt.

6 FIGHTING UNDER CONSTANT FIRE

One of the hard facts of life is that we usually don't get something unless we fight for it. Much of our potential to be happy depends on confronting situations and resolving them. Yet "confrontation" is used with a negative connotation. To call someone "confrontational" is not a compliment.

Do not be surprised at the need for confrontation. With 7 billion people in the world, there are bound to be plenty of antagonists. Accept that confrontation is part of life. Spending your energy on asking "Why do I have to deal with this difficult person?" is natural to ask, but only once – after that it is a drain. Instead, focus on how to remedy the situation.

Most of us have our first experience of confrontation when we are children, whether with peers or parents. As we are too young to know how to handle it at the time, we get the impression that confrontation is something to be avoided. As we get older and more mature, we learn all sorts of ways of avoiding confrontation and confrontational people.

I would guess that the vast majority of people reading this book are not particularly aggressive. We've developed a tendency to outwardly accept situations as they are, for fear of confronting them, and a tendency to be overly diplomatic. This inability to confront then haunts us later, when we have not achieved what we wanted.

CHALLENGES AND COURAGE

The challenge – and we should view problems as challenges – is to confront situations in a manner that is constructive and inoffensive, rather than destructive. Confrontation, and learning to do it properly, involves the three points of a classic prayer that you may have heard before: "God, please grant me the serenity to accept the things I cannot change, the courage to change the things I can, and the wisdom to know the difference." To confront a situation, we must have examined all possibilities; at the same time, we must do it without excess emotion; and of course, we must have the courage to take that step.

Courage is a misunderstood word. It is often seen as an absolute term, meaning "the complete absence of fear." But courage is not about *not* having fear; courage is about acknowledging fear and still making the decision to confront your difficulties. Tal Ben-Shahar, a pillar of the positive psychology movement, phrases it as "Courage is about having fear and going ahead anyway." A soldier or police officer *has* to feel fear in dangerous situations, or else he or she would act with no regard for their own lives. In the same way, our day-to-day challenges, whether being in charge of a project at work, leading an important meeting, or calling a client, can also awaken our fears. The question is whether or not we go ahead. We don't need to feel blind courage every time we make a decision, and of course there is a word for acting with courage while ignoring reason: "foolhardy."

Being able to fight also means being persistent. This was something I had to force myself to accept, as I never appreciated (or liked) persistence when I was in my depression. Sometimes, overcoming a difficulty is a long road. We need to tell ourselves that we will triumph, but that it's probably not going to happen immediately. The main thing is to not lose your faith in yourself. In the words of Winston Churchill, who saw his country bombed mercilessly for years during World War II: "If you're going through hell, keep going."

The ability to confront a difficulty goes along with one of the themes of this book: that Change can be a good thing. As someone who has suffered from anxiety and depression, I disliked the concept of change for many years, and took many steps to avoid confronting it. To me, change represented a lack of control, and the possibility – or in my mind, the *probability* – that things would get worse.

Ironically, I failed to see that my life, my circumstances, would only get better if there was Change. I had to confront my ingrained way of thinking and say to myself, "Tom, what you've been doing up to now simply hasn't worked. And if you don't make some changes now, you're going to be in the same situation in one year, five years, *ten* years from now."

FACING FACTS

As mentioned above, we cannot escape the fact that confrontation is part of life. As peaceful as we may wish to be, that sort of

> *Nothing gets accomplished without some sort of conflict.*

blissful peace, without confrontation, is for the afterlife. The world we live in is one of conflict, and we have to learn how to confront situations and to win. Otherwise, we will be walked over by those around us, and lead lives, in the words of Henry David Thoreau, of "quiet desperation." We want to accomplish things, don't we? Well nothing gets accomplished without some sort of conflict.

The first rule of learning to confront situations is: *Keep the passion, lose the emotion.* You will often see that the person who loses their temper is the

> *Keep the passion, lose the emotion.*

one who comes out losing. Second, make sure that you truly feel that you are right. Lastly, and this is crucial, avoid an "all-or-nothing" mentality. I suffered from this way of thinking for many years – "It's *my* way, or the highway" – and it never brought me any benefits. Along with confrontation, there must also be an ability to compromise.

Most of our confrontations are within us. Our "enemies" are described in each chapter: the past, anxiety, depression, overthinking, pride, etc. There are plenty of forces that do not want us to be happy. All we can do is fight them as best we can. Each needs to be handled in a slightly different way, but the essential strategy is to understand that these forces embed themselves in our mind and shape our thoughts and perceptions. As motivational speaker Jim Rohn said in a lecture from the 1980s, "All good will be attacked; every garden will be invaded." These enemies are not going to go away unless we force them out.

It's never too late to change from being a negative to a positive person. After you've told yourself, as you should each day, that you want and deserve to be happy, start training yourself for the daily battle. Do anything you can to be prepared. Eat right, exercise, try to learn new skills that will make you better at your job and more valuable. Most importantly, focus on the positive. Become more positive by being grateful for the good things in your life. That's how you train your mind. Positive people confront situations with confidence, and you will be one of these people. It's never too late to change from being a negative to a positive person.

7 THE PAST

History teachers have often said, "If we do not study the past, then we are doomed to repeat it." However, for the depressive person, recalling the past means re-living it. And unfortunately we choose to remember the bad things and focus on the negative.

Early in the 20th century, physicist Albert Einstein published his Theory of Relativity. The implications of the theory were various, and some are even still being discovered. However, one immediate implication, and one which was revolutionary, was that Time itself was a dimension – the Fourth Dimension. Einstein argued, successfully, that the time at which something occurs is as essential to its existence as length, width, or height.

I mention this not as a lesson in the history of physics, but to illustrate that the time at which things take place plays a crucial role in how and why we make decisions. Even when we feel that we are making the best decision, it is really just the best decision we can make *at that time*. It is so common for us to look back and say how foolish we've been, when really, at the time, we certainly didn't mean to be "foolish" at all.

THE PULL OF THE PAST

One of the chapters in J.R.R. Tolkien's *The Lord of the Rings* is titled "The Shadow of the Past". For many years, "the shadow of the past" was where I lived my life. My mind made constant references to past experiences. While some of these were enjoyable, generally most of the memories to which my mind resorted were unpleasant. I gradually realized that I had a serious problem.

Many of us live our lives this way, looking backward. It is ironic that the things that keep us from moving forward are the things that are already behind us. We know that we can't make the Earth spin backwards, like Superman, though somehow our minds ignore this simple law of physics and persist in dwelling on things that cannot ever be changed. As the Roman poet Persius said in the first century AD, "We consume our tomorrows fretting about our yesterdays."

Of all of the people that I know, I myself have always been the most guilty of allowing my past to dominate my present. I had made an abundance of poor choices by the time I was in my mid-20s. Choosing the wrong major in college, a failure to take my career as seriously as I should have, an overly hedonistic lifestyle – the list goes on. As I looked at these, I started going back to my early high school days, and even junior high, to question and criticize what I did. While doing so, I got wrapped up in all the emotional and psychological unpleasantness of those years.

This destructive rumination took place every day in my mind for nearly ten years. In terms of time, I spent a fortune thinking about things that were as impossible to change as making one plus one equal three. All of that time could have been spent enjoying the present and considering how to improve my life for the years ahead. To quote Churchill again, "If we open a quarrel between past and present, we shall find that we have lost the future."

It was not until I read Eckhart Tolle's extraordinary book *The Power of Now* that I began to view my life differently. The book begins with the line, "I have little use for the past and rarely think about it." This remains the most profound and meaningful statement I have *ever* read. I had always seen my life as completely dependent on my past, and in fact there really wasn't a "present" in my life psychologically – it was just the past and the future, the one filling me with depression and the other with anxiety. Notice the first part of Tolle's sentence: "I have little use for the past." He is right: the past does not have many uses, especially as it is unchangeable.

> *The past does not have many uses, especially as it is unchangeable.*

ACCEPTING THIS IMMUTABILITY

Life accustoms us to the idea of "fixing" things. Our entire childhoods and adolescence are based on being given problems in school that we are expected to solve. By the time we have reached adulthood, we have the belief, both consciously and subconsciously, that there's a solution to everything. And then we encounter the past.

Most people, by the time they reach 25, have a number of negative things in their past which they wish they could change. These could be poor academic performance, the wrong choice of college or career, bad relationship decisions – or even some things that didn't involve choices, like an unhappy childhood. From ages 0 to 18, it can be said that our "past" has not really solidified yet into an entity; but as we get older and make more important decisions – decisions which are irreparable – the past becomes its own entity, a distinct part of our lives. And, as adults who want our lives to be better in the present, we are tempted to think we can change the past.

The phrase "nothing is impossible" has entered popular culture, and it accords with what we are taught in our youth. But let's face reality: some things *are* impossible. One plus one cannot equal three; a rock cannot walk; and the past cannot be changed. It's as simple as that. Once you accept that changing the past is as impossible as breaking a law of mathematics or physics, you are on your way to decreasing the amount of time you spend dwelling on it.

Unless time-travel becomes a reality, it is impossible to revisit the past; and even if we could "travel time," the world would not last a day without being completely altered, corrupted, and destroyed. Life is *linear*: it consists of the present moving into the future. To go against this current is to go against nature.

> **Thinking about the past is no ticket to a happy present or future.**

I do not take Tolle's quote to an extreme – one still has to acknowledge the past from time to time. I am willing to talk about my past if I meet someone who has lived in the same places that I have, or who went to one of the same schools. But I do not proactively talk about it. When I find myself drifting into the past, I repeat Tolle's line like a mantra.

Training yourself to ignore the past is a challenge, partly because the past does have its positive aspects, such as happy moments, successes, etc. Unfortunately, if you want to escape the trap of the past, you need to treat the past by ignoring it. In time, as you get healthier and more positive in your thinking, your mind will allow you to visit those happy memories. Don't worry, they will still be there. But you need to establish a forward, linear current to your thoughts that leads you away from the past, as thinking about the past will not help you to be a happier person. Your mind can train itself, if you try. When you catch yourself going back to the past, tell yourself to stay in the present, and, as I do, repeat Tolle's sentence to yourself. Accept that thinking about the past is no ticket to a happy present or future.

THE TORTURE OF REFLECTION

As stated above, our education teaches us that reflection is important, as it helps us to digest and learn from what has happened. However, there is a sharp distinction between constructive reflection and destructive reflection. The first means looking at an experience you have had, learning from it, and moving on -- using what you've learned to help your present. The second type, destructive reflection, means entrapping yourself in the hamster-wheel of the past, second-guessing and multi-guessing your actions, and not moving forward at all.

Save reflection for the wisdom of old age. Save reflection for the wisdom of old age. Lord Beaverbrook, in an essay simply titled "Calm," states that "Old age is the time for looking back on the pleasures and achievements of the past – when success or failure may seem matters of comparative unimportance." Prior to this comfortable and wise time of life, especially for the negativist or depressive, reflecting on good things soon turns to nostalgia, wishing that you could relive those moments with that person or place, or of that time of your life -- and this soon leads to the sad realization that you cannot. It can also lead to picking that good memory apart and finding negative aspects or forming negative conclusions.

I have never met a successful or happy person who talked much about their past, if at all. People who are happy and successful are focused on the present as well as the future. They don't spend time – which is irreplaceable -- lamenting past failures or celebrating past successes.

THE WAY FORWARD

You cannot see the light if you are looking at your shadow. Always keep in mind that you cannot see the light if you are looking at your shadow. To advance in life, in your self-improvement, in your path to fulfillment and peace of mind, you cannot look back on what has already happened. The past, whether positive or negative, can be seductive in its pull, but it hurls you backwards and downhill. Meanwhile, time is moving forward, so you are mentally moving in the wrong direction while time marches on. Beat yourself up over the past, and you will relive it into the future.

Reflectiveness, and an obsession with the past, are psychological issues that it is difficult to fight against with any complex strategy. The way to combat them is through the brute force of telling yourself to ignore them, and with Tolle's quote. It has definitely worked for me.

8 OVERTHINKING

Overthinking is a little-known symptom of being unhappy – and also a frequently ignored cause. It is dangerous because "thinking" is looked at in such a positive light. Few imagine an excess of thinking to be harmful. Children are always being told to think more, and a frequent criticism heard is "You just don't *think* sometimes."

The inability to stop thinking – *thinkaholism* – is dangerous for a variety of reasons. For one, it makes life complicated; two, it causes inaction; and three, it drives you back into the past -- the negative past.

Overthinking has been a bane to me all my life, and the worst part is that I always thought it was an asset. I grew up idolizing real-life people like Albert Einstein, and fictional characters like Sherlock Holmes and Doctor Who, all of whom were portrayed as putting a lot of emphasis on sheer *thinking*. Perhaps the reason for this was that my mind never seemed to stop, and I likened myself to these individuals.

It was a surprise to me when I learned that not everyone has the problem of overthinking. For most of my life, I had thought it was normal. Our culture venerates thinking, as seen in literature, the study of philosophy, the respect given to the concept of the "absent-minded professor," and most tangibly in the statue of The Thinker, by Rodin. Our culture is not prepared to consider that overthinking is a factor in many people's unhappiness.

However, the fact is that too much of anything is bad for you, and this rule certainly applies to thinking. The mind, like a muscle, is not meant to be flexed nonstop for 17

The mind is not meant to be flexed nonstop for 17 hours a day.

hours a day. "Blessed are they who don't think too much," I have often said. When you engage in excessive thought, you are psychologically propelled backwards, and begin thinking and reflecting negatively.

Asking "Why?"

Western culture teaches us to ask "Why?", and young children are famous for using the word repeatedly. One of my friends finally limited his toddler son to five "whys" at a time!

We ask "why" because it is against our culture to simply accept things. We want to know why there are certain rules, why things are the way they are, why we have to do something that we don't want to do. In many ways, this is a positive thing that has often led to discovery.

Nevertheless, we must also keep in mind that there are a lot of instances in life in which we have to accept a situation as it is. Death is the most obvious of these, and so is the past. The past cannot be changed; it is written in the stone of time, and we have to accept the decisions that we made and the actions that we committed, and then live with them.

"Why did I study a major that doesn't lead to a job?" Is that question worth asking, once you've graduated? No – instead, spend your mental energy on seeing what you can do to make things better. Take a vocational course, go to night school, and look into how your skills and major can overlap with industries where there are jobs and money. Yes, we have to "live with" our bad decisions, but that doesn't mean we cannot make the best of them. We'll discuss asking "Why?" and curiosity further in a later chapter.

OVERTHINKING AND DEPRESSION

While I am a strong advocate of having time alone, prolonged periods of solitude lead to overthinking, and overthinking then leads to depression. Most depressives have idealized about living on a desert island. The fact is that being alone and bored would be the worst thing for a depressive.

Even the happiest memory can be "overthought" into being a bad one.

An inclination to pondering, to rumination, is part of anxiety, depression, guilt, shame, and nearly all aspects of being unhappy. The mind is a powerful weapon, but in cases like depression, it begins to act against you when it is overused. Even the happiest memory can be "overthought" into being a bad one.

While I strongly admired "deep thinkers," the distinction which I failed to make was that these individuals generally did not pursue "idle" thinking – that is, thinking without a specific purpose. Their minds were constantly fixed on solving a particular problem. Sherlock Holmes, while fictional, is an interesting study, as he lapses into depression when he does not have a problem to solve. He then, sadly, resorts to narcotics. Holmes is a thinkaholic, and not a particularly happy man.

CURTAILING OVERTHINKING

My happiest days have been those in which I was able to think when I wanted to think, and rest my mind when I wanted it to rest. Prior to learning this skill, my best days where the ones in which I could focus on one problem. Although I found mathematics difficult, I also found it relaxing, as it forced me to focus. In contrast, when I have not been compelled to concentrate, I have suffered days of descending into the depths of thought, and dwelling on the past, my failures, and my shortcomings. Finally I despaired and said, "If only we cut shut the mind off!" The truth is that in many ways, we can.

Although I believe that a tendency towards overthinking is inborn, in many ways it has similar qualities to a bad habit. Hence, like bad habits, it can be tamed and even broken. The process begins by recognizing that you overthink. How can we differentiate between thinking and overthinking? One easy way is to compare it to over-exercising or overeating: it reaches a point at which it is tiring you and harming you. Less physically, another way to measure it is to examine the purposefulness of your thinking. When you find that your thinking is not focused, and that it is nonlinear, it means you are overthinking. Thoughts that are goal-oriented are good; thoughts that have no goal at all, are not.

So where do we actually start? I'll admit that it is one of the more difficult challenges to overcome. With overexercising, you can simply refrain from going to the gym. But how can you control your own mind?

Naturally, simply telling your mind to stop thinking is not effective. Try, right now, to *not* imagine a helicopter flying directly over you. I'm sure you just mentally pictured it, and may have even "heard" it!

Let's begin by admitting that despite your tendency to overthink, there will occasionally be moments of non-thinking. These will be few, but they will exist. When they happen, tell your mind "Thank you." I know it sounds strange, but go ahead and do it. So often we are saying to ourselves, "Think! Think!" Hence, it follows that we should also be able to encourage the mind to appreciate non-thinking. What happens by thanking the mind, is that the mind starts to learn what pleases you. It is strange to think that the different parts of the mind can communicate with each other, but why not? Different parts of the mind communicate with different parts of the body.

PHYSICAL REMEDIES

Responsive as the mind is, it's never going to fully stop thinking – certainly not for long periods of time. The more we can enforce periods where the mind is focused on a goal, the more we can keep it from its tendency to crawl into the past with that negative flow.

As mentioned earlier, with regard to lifting weights I advise against the use of heavy weight that requires a lot of rest time between sets. This "rest time" is just time in which you can get lost in rumination. If you are fond of weights, do sets that involve a lot of repetitions. For myself, I begin each day with four sets of at least 50 pushups. During this workout, all I am focused on is getting through the set, then catching my breath, and then doing the next set. My brain doesn't have time to get lost in any thoughts.

A general rule is to do physical exercises that are of medium length. For runners, bear in mind that long distances will involve periods of equilibrium where you will have too much time to think. Rather, choose a run that requires you to constantly be conscious of the running itself, and which constantly challenges you. This can be envisioned as a "long sprint."

Again, each time you realize you are not thinking and ruminating, thank your mind for this.

NONPHYSICAL REMEDIES

For nonphysical remedies, I recommend something that keeps your mind active but focused. Reading is not a good remedy, as there is a strong probability that the mind will wander. As someone who loves reading, this was a difficult challenge for me to overcome, and my solution was to give myself a 20-30 minute chunk of time in which to read a certain amount. Television, especially some of the series that have come out over the past ten years, is better at keeping one's attention. These series, while somewhat addictive, do have the effect of distracting the mind and preventing overthinking. These series will not have a profound effect on your happiness in the long term, but they are an excellent distraction for when you cannot stop your mind from ruminating.

As for crossword puzzles and video games, bear in mind that these introduce frustrations that may likely render you agitated. I don't recommend them.

One pleasant act, that has always helped to keep my mind active and focused, is writing letters -- these days, in the form of emails -- to family and friends. In letters, we tend to focus on the positive, and to think of how much we like the person we are writing to. These are two very positive and helpful things. Writing in a journal can also help. For days when I find myself overthinking, I take a few minutes and send myself an email full of whatever is on my mind. My mind is then relieved of worrying about these topics.

Conversation is a wonderful aid to the pain of an overactive mind.

Another means of combating overthinking is to be around people. Conversation, with its need for quick responses, is a wonderful aid to the pain of an overactive mind. It would be great if the robots of the future — who apparently will clean our houses and cook our meals – would be excellent conversationalists! Prolonged solitude, as discussed, is not helpful to the overthinker. If, for some reason, you are in a situation where you cannot be with a conversation companion, at least go out and be in the midst of nature and humanity. When in doubt, be in motion.

As mentioned in my chapter on The Past, I also highly advise getting a copy of Tolle's *The Power of Now*, which contains guidance on combating rumination.

9   Guilt

Entwined with a fixation on the past is the potential for extreme feelings of guilt. I use "guilt" in the sense of self-reproach. For many years, I considered myself free from guilt, but as I got older, it hit me like an avalanche.

To begin, I'd like to state the distinction here between Guilt and Shame. Guilt is an internal feeling of self-blame, while shame is much more related to external circumstances. Shame usually refers to the way one feels perceived by another person or group of people.

There are also "guilt" cultures and "shame" cultures. Western civilization is mainly a "guilt" culture, in which we are taught and raised to feel guilt when we have hurt someone. It is a product of Christian teaching – the concept that we are responsible for treating others as we want to be treated.

In contrast, the Eastern countries, especially the Far East, are "shame" cultures: feeling bad about an action comes from others seeing it or knowing about it. It is directly related to the concept of "face," which permeates Asian cultures very thoroughly.

That is not to say that both cultures do not experience both feelings. But it is not surprising that the West, which is more individualistic, is inclined towards guilt, while the East, in which cultures are more collective, is inclined towards Shame.

PERSONAL GUILT

To start with a personal story, I experienced feelings of guilt for many years over the person I was when I was a teen. In high school I aspired to be #1 in my class and totally independent, and my only desire was to get a scholarship to college. Of course, it is good to have goals; however, I allowed my relentless pursuit of academic perfection to have a destructive effect on my relationship with family members. I became an unbearable person to be around, especially to live with, and I know that I made my family's life harder during this period. I also sacrificed friendships and the development of social skills that would be necessary for college and for life. In the end, I did get to be #1 in my class, and I did get the scholarship, but the damage had been done. Looking at the person I had to become in order to achieve this scholarship, it was indeed a Pyrrhic victory, as mentioned above.

My guilt over how I treated people during high school did not start to surface till years later, when I became a mature man. Guilt is indeed a sign of maturity, and has some positive sides, in that it signifies we have a sense of what is right and wrong – an internal sense of judgment.

Guilt is a sign of maturity, but can be an all-consuming force.

Unfortunately, it can be an all-consuming force, especially as the source of our guilt has often passed out of our control.

> *If you can't forgive yourself, you will have trouble forgiving others.*

I have said that my high school days caused me the most guilt, but the feeling of guilt feeds on itself, and can take you back into the past. Guilt combines with overthinking, and *overthinking makes everything worse.* The more that it occupied my mind, the more it took me farther back, and I realized that there were things from childhood that I hadn't yet forgiven myself for. Learning to forgive yourself is the first step in a larger challenge to happiness, that of learning to forgive others.

Why is self-forgiveness so difficult? Largely because of the way that we are raised. We are taught that forgiveness has to be granted to us by another person, whether a parent, teacher, or priest.

I carried around self-resentment for years, until I finally said, "enough is enough." We will discuss resentment and forgiveness more in a later chapter, but for now, let's look at a case study involving guilt.

ALAN'S CASE

One story of relentless guilt that comes immediately to mind is that of another American I met while travelling. Alan – not his real name – had an estranged relationship with his parents in his 20s, and was also a severe drug addict at the time. He had a bit of money, and one day decided to leave the US and go on a trip to South America and Europe. As he was a heavy drug user, this ended up being a half-year "bender" in which he experimented with a variety of narcotics, losing himself thoroughly in the drug scene. This was in the days before cell phones, Facebook, and email, and he didn't bother to call home or tell his family where he was.

When Alan did return back to the US, he found out that while he had been out of the country, his father had been diagnosed with Stage 4 stomach cancer and, with the rapid progression of the disease, had passed away. His father had died knowing that his only son was a drug addict, and thinking that his son didn't care about him – or perhaps even that he didn't love him.

The Alan that I met was no longer a drug addict, but he was full of feelings of guilt that had lasted for years. I hadn't actually known him long, before he told me his story. In his eyes there was a sense of searching. He was mature enough to know how much he had hurt his father and his family; he hadn't been there at their time of need, or even expressed any concern. However, now that his father had died, he couldn't even apologize to him in person.

Many of us have aspects of our past that give us feelings of guilt. In Alan's case, it was impossible to repair his behavior "directly" with his father, who had passed away. What Alan had to realize, most of all, was that you cannot let guilt rule your life. While there was no way that Alan could communicate with his father, I advised him to "apologize" by doing things that would make his dad proud: to be kind and attentive towards his sister and nephew, and his mother; to do good to others (his father had been involved in charity work); overall, to act in ways that would have made his father proud of him. As you cannot do the impossible, you do whatever is possible. When Alan did finally raise his feelings of guilt with his family, he realized that they had long forgiven him. It was he who had been unable to forgive himself.

DON'T REGRET. REDEEM.

> *We can spend our lives regretting our actions, but how does this help anyone, including ourselves?*

I offer a simple message: "Don't regret. Redeem." We can spend our lives regretting our actions, but how does this help anyone, including ourselves? As I learned while talking with Alan, and with many others since, redemption need not be direct. The world offers us a tremendous amount of opportunities to do good deeds. Poverty alleviation, economic empowerment, and anything that aids progress, are ways of redeeming oneself. The thousands or perhaps even millions of mistakes that I have made in the past cannot all be atoned for directly, but I feel much better about myself when I work with charities or even do a meaningful favor for someone. Transfer your guilt into doing good deeds, rather than torturing yourself.

10 "ME" TIME, AND TIME WITH OTHERS

Ben Franklin, whose interests and triumphs lay in more areas than can be concisely listed here, was an exemplar of the principle that all time should be used wisely. "Do not squander time, for that's the stuff life is made of," was one of his many precepts. While Franklin discouraged "down time," in his period there were inevitable periods for rest and recovery. The sun set at 6pm, and there was no TV or Internet. You had "down time" whether you wanted it or not.

The 21st century is the exact opposite. We are constantly being contacted with emails, tweets, text messages, and a myriad of other forms of communication. I personally have Skype, email, Linked in, Facebook, WeChat, and Whatsapp, and my friends make fun of me for not having Viber. How much do I need?

Technology has done many excellent things, but it has not helped in decreasing stress levels. We are currently living in the most distracting and complicated age since the dawn of mankind. At the same time, it is also the least physically-demanding. This is a bad combination. In this day and age, more than ever, we have to be proactive in seeking simplicity.

Like it or not, technology is here to stay, so the objective is to find how you can be a happy, smoothly functioning person in an increasingly complex world.

SOLITUDE

Solitude, which simply means the state of being alone, has come under a lot of criticism in recent years. It is viewed by many as being equivalent to being antisocial, introverted (another word with a negative connotation), and self-absorbed. People have a concept that solitude is caused by negative feelings, and that it is a cause of depression.

The fact is that all of us need an element of solitude in our lives. It varies from person to person, across genders and across cultures. John Gray, in his excellent *Men are from Mars, Women are from Venus*, describes how men need to "go into their cave" at times, as a way of dealing with frustration or failure. With women, the reasons and benefits of solitude are slightly different, and solitude doesn't seem to have as much of a curative effect on unhappiness as with men. Culturally, Anglo-Saxon culture is the most understanding of solitude, though many still consider it to be negative, whereas as one goes further East, the simple idea of being alone strikes an uncomfortable note; eating alone is almost unheard of, and living alone is uncommon.

The main benefit of solitude is that it enables you to recharge, and that it allows you to be *you*. Whether or not you enjoy being sociable, you cannot always be "yourself" when you are among others – and this can become tiring. We all need space in our lives, to varying degrees. As stated above, men generally need to have more space than women. Men's nature craves a period of time where he can recharge and "regroup"; to think

> *Solitude allows you to recharge, and allows you to be YOU.*

(but not overthink) without interruption; to not have the pressure of responding to questions or of making decisions. It is a period of time which we feel we deserve, and it is also a time for discovery. Time with ourselves allows us to develop our thoughts and consolidate what we feel is worth doing with our energy and interests. "Look within," says Marcus Aurelius. "Within is the fountain of good, and it will ever bubble up, if you will ever dig."

Truly uninterrupted solitude has become a challenge to find. While we may be physically solitary, we are not alone digitally or technologically. As mentioned above, the list of ways in which we can be reached is exhausting, and those who are sending messages are increasingly impatient for replies. It is an age in which one has to be diligent and proactive in finding "me" time.

But it is possible. I have always found that the hours of the early morning have less digital "traffic." Even so, I have had to fight for my solitude. For the past few years, Sunday mornings for me have been sacrosanct. My phone is on silent, I don't check my messages, and I don't look at my emails – in fact, I don't go near my computer till noon. I am "off-grid." And during this time, I am catching up on my reading, writing, cleaning, exercising, occasionally watching television – it really doesn't matter. The point is that I am free from the need to continually be responsive and make decisions. It is a great joy just to know that for four or five hours, I have this freedom and restfulness.

Just as bodies need to spend time apart from each other, so do minds. People who do not live alone will find solitude difficult to achieve. There is the inclination for a spouse to assume that "something's wrong" when their other half doesn't want to talk. And this need for solitude should be addressed. It may sound unromantic, but it is not good if a couple has no time away from each other. The simple reason is that we have been created as individuals, with individual DNA and bodies. Just as bodies need to spend time apart from each other, so do minds.

If you do not live alone, and cannot attain solitude within your home, find a sanctuary. The main qualifications are a place that is quiet, with no or minimal people, and few or no distractions. Thus, I would rule out a bar and even coffee shops, though the latter are acceptable if you can find a quiet spot where you won't be disturbed. Some suggestions:

- A library: an ideal place, as phone calls are discouraged, silence is required, and there are plenty of books.

- *Not* the office. Even when no one is there. The temptation to do work, the possibility of your boss or colleagues coming in, means you will not be relaxed.

- If you are outdoorsy, find a place in the woods, or by a flowing river, where you can sit. You will have to have an alternative to this for when the weather is inclement.

- Restaurants and diners: get a booth table, and as long as you order something, you are generally left alone.

To increase your potential for peace of mind, choose a period per week when you can have a few hours of "me" time. This is not time to be spent in idle rumination, which is one of our enemies. Rather, it is just time where the social part of the mind can rest. You will find yourself refreshed when you later go out to be sociable. Sunday mornings may not work for everyone, but that's why Saturdays are there.

TIME WITH OTHERS

In the 1600s, the poet John Donne wrote that "No man is an island." It was at a time where the Renaissance was giving a new dimension to human capability, a time in which knowledge had been unearthed from being buried during the Middle Ages. What Donne was saying, was that despite all of the academic knowledge that we were accumulating, we were still part of humanity -- part of society and civilization. Sir Francis Bacon, another intellectual of the time, wrote that "To spend too much time in studies is sloth." People need to be around others, and part of feeling fulfilled is contributing to the society in which one lives.

Human nature has been constructed in such a way that the society of others is essential to our wellbeing. True, there are days in which we would prefer to be on a desert island, like Robinson Crusoe, and away from all humanity. However, one thing that the story of *Robinson Crusoe* demonstrates is that although you can create – through Reason and hard work --- a sustainable *existence* for yourself that is solitary, you cannot create much of a *life*. For the latter, you need other people, as Crusoe did.

In my unhappiest times, I have run for solitude to find peace of mind. However, in most cases, what ultimately enabled me to arise to a state of happiness was talking and laughing with others, and freeing my mind from constantly revisiting my troubles. Peace of mind was the foundation on which my happiness was built. More to come on that.

FRIENDS

As mentioned in the Introduction, I began to undergo a serious depression in my early 30s. I descended into it unknowingly, and experienced the "tunnel vision" that I discussed earlier. To me, in my tunnel, I was seeing the world as it was. To others, I was being extremely negative and pessimistic about everything. My friends, while not arranging an "intervention" to tell me this, individually told me that I sounded very unhappy and negative. One even suggested that I should seek professional therapy. It took courage for them to say this, and that is a quality that we look for in our friendships.

It is great to have friends who listen to you when you are feeling down, and who express an interest in helping you through your problems. On top

> *One of the responsibilities of a close friend is to challenge you at times.*

of that, it is even better when your friends challenge you – when they don't just agree with you. Sometimes, we need to be re-focused or told that we are wrong. Awkward as it may be at times, one of the responsibilities of a close friend is to challenge you at times.

I've often heard the phrase "Stay away from negative people," but this needs to be qualified. Negative people are in need of help. I was fortunate that my friends did not abandon me, and I myself believe in sticking by friends when they start to see the world through the lens of pessimism. Negativity, as stated before, is a matter of perspective, and perspective can be changed.

Friends can be an excellent source of wisdom, and throughout my adulthood, I have had the benefit of several friends who were significantly older. I've found that as people get older, they become better listeners. In the other direction, older friends have told me that that they enjoy the company of younger people, as it keeps them young! For some reason, age groups don't seem to mix well in Western countries, though as an expatriate, it was common for me to have friends who were twice my age.

For business, an appreciation for *people* is essential. The phrase "self-made millionaire" ignores the fact that no one

> *Powerful people accept the reality that they need others.*

becomes successful completely on their own, and I've never met a successful person who attributed all of his success to himself. Powerful people accept the reality that they need others – often more than most people. Imagine a king without his army, or a successful entrepreneur without her team. Indeed, no man is an island.

A QUICK NOTE ON BEING BUSY

When I was young, in the 1980s, the typical response to "How are you" was "Fine." Over the past two decades, the most common response has been "Busy" or "Very busy." It is a sign of the times, but also significant, that we talk more about our activity than about how we actually feel. I try to phrase my greetings to people in ways that allow them to answer more interestingly: *What did you do over the weekend?*, *What did you do last night?* And so forth. We're *all* "busy" these days – so why bother saying it?

Not that there is anything essentially wrong with being busy, as long as it is with a purpose. (Note that "busy" does not mean being "crazy busy," as in talking on two phones at once and rushing to meeting after meeting.) For those who suffer from depression and negativity, being busy is a much better alternative to being bored or idle. The mind needs something to focus on, or it will turn on itself.

11 USING ENTERTAINMENT

While in several parts of this book I discuss using exercise to assist in self-improvement, I'd like to talk about non-physical remedies here – specifically, forms of entertainment.

HUMOR

When you are in "negative mode," humor initially seems impractical, useless, and unproductive. However, humor and laughter

> *Humor and laughter help rebuild your positive "qi."*

help rebuild your positive "qi." *Qi* is a Chinese term that can be translated as a "life energy force." Over the centuries, we have forgotten about the essential element and purpose of humor, which was to make people forget their troubles and to put troubles into a manageable framework. Its importance to mental and spiritual health has been trivialized, and it is now largely seen as a sub-sector of Hollywood. The restorative powers of humor have largely been forgotten.

Kings had special court employees called "fools," but fools were not there just for sheer entertainment. The Fool often spoke a kind of wisdom. Kings suffered from extreme bouts of negativity, anxiety, and depression, due to their almost endless responsibilities, threats of rebellion and invasion, and the constant need to make decisions. Having a provider of humor was a way of restoring positive *qi*.

It is surprising that humor is not a more significant part of our lives. Humor costs nothing, and produces laughter, which, if not the best medicine, certainly makes us feel better. As adults, we are always trying to make children laugh, as it means that they are feeling happy. So why doesn't this approach carry over into adulthood?

Seeing how humor does elevate our spirits, and help us to forget our troubles, one would think that companies would have mandatory "humor sessions" – they could even bring in a comedian, for example. But no: with the increasing busyness of our lives, humor has been relegated to something that is either unimportant or negligible.

There are several reasons for this. One is that we have become so overwhelmed with digital technology, and the need to keep up with the next email. Another is that humor is seen as not taking something seriously enough; bosses view it as immature and a waste of time. The perception of humor and laughter is that they are purely recreational; despite the adage that "laughter is the best medicine," society, especially the working world, disregards its medicinal and restorative properties. The hypersensitivity of the 1990s has also not helped. Jokes now have to be neutral and inoffensive, and people are more uptight than in the past 100 years.

Using Humor

But this is not an academic study on the history of humor, but rather an exploration of how we can use humor as a weapon in the fight to be happy. I first discovered its usefulness in high school, when I was obsessed with high grades. With the stress that I had, to be #1 in my class, I needed relief; and this came in the form of *The Simpsons* and *Seinfeld*, arguably the two most successful comedy shows of the 1990s. In college, my friends and I would take a break from our studies every day at 7pm to watch *The Simpsons*. What I realized was that in addition to the show being funny, it also brought all of us together. After the show would finish, we would linger for another half hour or so, repeating the jokes and also discussing how our days went and what we were working on. The high spirits which we were in, due to the show, helped us to feel revived, particularly for an assignment or exam that we were facing.

We are blessed to be living in an age where finding something humorous to watch is just a click away. Make laughter a required part of your day.

> *Make laughter a required part of your day.*

You can even make it the first thing you do. When you wake up, if you are feeling depressed, watch a funny show on TV or the Internet. You can also listen to it in the car or train on the way to work, perhaps even on your lunch hour.

And lunch hours are for rest, not for work. If you only have half an hour, don't use it for work, and don't eat a sandwich at your desk. Lunchtime is *not* just about food.

SARCASM

One of the first things I've always done when moving to another country was find out its culture's sense of humor. Humor differs from country to country, as well as from region to region. Growing up in the American northeast, close to New York City, I was exposed to a very verbal and often sarcastic type of humor that is not shared by most of the remainder of the country. Middle America is a slightly more serious place, with a lower tolerance for racy humor. Internationally, the English have one of the wittiest senses of humor that can be found.

Sarcasm is anger's ugly cousin. Sarcasm, as described in the film *Anger Management*, starring Jack Nicholson and Adam Sandler, is "anger's ugly cousin." It takes humor and corrupts it with negativity, like taking a sweet food and tarnishing it with bitterness. As I got deeper into a depression, it was a British friend who remarked that sarcasm had become my general response to everything, and that it sounded negative rather than funny. For a long time, this sarcastic streak was on the list of things I wanted to change about myself.

I also noticed that as I became more negative, I felt that I was somehow "distorting reality" if I allowed humor to cheer me up. The fact is that my perspective already *was* distorted – I had "tunnel vision." It was a critical error. Humor shows you -- *reminds* you -- that a positive side of life does indeed exist; that people can help you feel better about yourself. It reinforces the idea that socializing is essential to our recovery; it provides relief to anxiety.

YOUR "HUMOR RESERVOIR"

The more humor that you expose yourself to, the more you fill your humor reservoir. This is the well that we go to when we are feeling down, and when we need to cheer up quickly in time for a meeting or social appointment. Everyone should have at least three very humorous memories that they can go to on a moment's notice, when they are under attack from depression or negativity. These can be memories of actual events or remembrances of funny scenes in movies, TV shows, or books. There is a line from *The Simpsons,* and a joke made by a colleague several years ago, that are permanently in my humor reservoir.

A SUBTLE ENEMY

So many of us start our day with the News, which is as depressing as any work of fiction -- and even more so, as it is about real life. A typical news broadcast features murders, accidents, war, and politics. No wonder we say "no news is good news." (Actually, there is plenty of good news out there -- plenty of charity work and scientific advances.) And after listening to the news, we go into a day of work! Later we return home after a tough day, and watch the news again. Where is the humor? Where is the relief from all the seriousness?

I'm not saying that we should ignore the news, but I do argue that those of us with depressive tendencies should be cautious of our intake of it. Further misery is not good company. If you are in a state of depression and negativity, my advice is to not watch the news or listen to it. Limit yourself to checking it online, at your own will. Keep it to a minimum.

MUSIC

Poet Percy Shelley wrote that "Music, when soft voices die, vibrates in the memory." The existence of music has never been explained. In many ways, it is not an "essential" part of everyday human life, yet it comes to us naturally, and across all cultures. It is something related to the human spirit, and hence it is here for us to enjoy and to use for self-improvement.

While I have my preferences, I have been fortunate to have an appreciation for various kinds of music. What I have learned is that there are different kinds of music for different occasions, particularly for someone who is trying to attain peace of mind and happiness. These days we can even download recordings of the ocean waves – some of which last for up to ten hours!

I recall one instance in my 20s, when I came home from work very angry. A client had changed their mind after a long saga of negotiations, and had been quite rude about it. As soon as I got home, I put on the most violent heavy metal song I could find, with lyrics about anger and vengeance, and felt the adrenaline of the song course through my veins. The song, in its words and instrumentation, represented what I was feeling, and the emotions that I'd had to contain with the client.

Music with a message of destruction and revenge can be useful on isolated occasions, where it serves as a harmless expression for your anger. However, it is not the music to listen to on a daily basis, particularly for individuals trying to develop peace in their lives. As Shelley says, music stays in the memory. You want to be careful about what types of songs enter your conscious and especially your subconscious mind. The subconscious plays a large, though unclear, role in our thinking.

TELEVISION AND MOVIES

In a similar vein, we should be careful of the other recreational aids we ingest. Television is one that immediately springs to mind. I recall watching one HBO series and realizing that it was so bleak as to be affecting my mood. You don't need TV to tell you that there are other people out there who are unhappy or depressed. At the same time, watching shows that reinforce your tunnel vision that the world is a negative place gives you a false sense of feeling comfortable in your view. You cannot achieve happiness if you think that the world is sad and terrible.

Unfortunately, many of the morose shows are also intelligent and well-written. If you do follow a bleak show, try to confine it to one series, and then try to counterbalance it with something lighthearted. I have already discussed humor, which I believe is indispensable. Although I am not a huge fan of game shows, I will gladly admit that they are agents of good feelings. Someone always wins, there is lots of applause, and along the way there are jokes and a positive momentum. For me, watching Steve Harvey on *Family Feud* is a great way to lighten my mood, and *Jeopardy* keeps me focused and even educated. Again, moderation is essential, and you don't need to watch a game show every day, but they are an easy antidote to the melancholy seen in many other TV programs.

One final way of integrating entertainment into your path to happiness is to make a list of the things that you enjoy. As I did, you will probably start with the very basic things, but as time goes on, you will start to realize how many little things in life are enjoyable. Hence, keep adding to your list, and do not make it general, but rather, ultra-specific. I ended up having all sorts of categories and sub-categories: different foods, different songs, even favorite aromas! In my depression, I had never thought of how pleasurable it is to smell coffee in the morning, or fresh-cut grass.

> *There is no limit on the amount of things that we can enjoy in life.*

Thankfully, there is no limit on the amount of things that we can enjoy in life. So start making your list!

12   THE HEDONISM TRAP

Very few depressives and negativists consciously choose to be hedonists. Rather, hedonism is their desperate way of dealing with their mental state. It is no coincidence that the lowest point in my depression was also the highest point in my hedonism.

In our lack of peace of mind and of positive thinking, we choose options that delight us, albeit for short periods of time. Ultimately, all of these options are taken to excess, as they are destructive distractions from our unhappiness, rather than remedies. At first, they have the same effect as a painkiller drug. In time, they are more similar to poison.

Hedonism becomes a trap because we begin to see excessive alcohol, drugs, sex, tobacco, and even eating as a way of life, and a way that is justified because it takes us away from the pain. Meanwhile, these excesses are diminishing our capabilities and taking us further off the rails.

James Allen, a self-help author from the early 1900s, whose *As a Man Thinketh* is still read (and available for free online), writes that "A man whose first thought is bestial indulgence could neither think clearly nor plan methodically; he could not find and develop his latent resources . . . he is not in a position to control affairs and adopt serious responsibilities."

Aside from the deterioration of the mind and body, hedonism also corrodes one's personality. I hesitate to say "character" here, but one's personality becomes impatient, dismissive, and unwilling to adopt new things. Anything that is challenging becomes viewed as boring and pointless. In this vein, hedonism blinded me to aspiring for more. When you can receive gratification instantaneously, such as from alcohol, you lose respect for the types of achievements that require long-term investment. Soon, your brain stops to even think about them. Life becomes a pursuit of hedonism, punctuated by periods called "work," where you need to earn money just to support your recreational habits.

"Chastise thy passions, that they avenge not themselves upon thee," says the philosopher Epictetus. This notion is seconded one generation later, by Marcus Aurelius, who states that "Pleasure can be one's overthrow. Instead, pursue magnanimity, simplicity, and equanimity."

> *Hedonism is never a substitute for peace of mind.*

Hedonism is never a substitute for peace of mind. It masks itself as positivity, when in reality it is self-deception. It is a dangerous form of escapism, because it becomes a way of life, and an addictive one. Cicero, another member of the ancient philosophical world, sums it up with color: "The unhappy man is mad with lust, indulging his ravenous appetites with insatiate greed, and the deeper he drinks of the most exquisite pleasures, the more parched with unquenchable thirst be becomes."

So Where Do We Draw the Line?

When does the devotion to pleasure become "excessive"? When anything that takes you away from it, no matter how useful or helpful to your life, is seen as an annoyance. Again, the deepest point in my depression was also when my hedonism was at its worst. The mere act of sending a letter at the post office was viewed through the hedonistic lens, and seen as too boring to do. Somehow, staying at home and flipping through channels on the TV, or going to a bar, seemed more productive.

To climb out of depression, many things are required, and one of these is less reliance on short-term pleasures. It may initially feel good to get drunk for several days on end, but eventually this loses its luster, and on top of that you are left with less money, weaker health, and perhaps an impaired professional life. The person who is feeling depressed needs to adopt a practice of self-discipline, of strengthening the mind and the body. It is easy to be self-destructive because you are depressed and may feel that you don't want to prolong your life. Nevertheless, in the back of your mind you know that you want to live, and that there are many positive and enjoyable things in the world (which you have listed in a previous chapter).

There's no point in leading yourself down a path to self-destruction, when you know you really want to improve

> *Every hedonistic outlet has an equal and self-improving counterpart.*

yourself and your life. Hedonism is often misplaced frustration, and such frustration can be channeled through exercise. If you must overeat, overeat on fruits and vegetables. For laughter, choose a funny film rather than a bottle of liquor. Every hedonistic outlet has an equal and self-improving counterpart.

13 BEING SURPRISED AT BAD THINGS

Nothing is stranger than life. The most fanciful science fiction, the most imaginative work of fantasy, cannot equal the unpredictability that surrounds every day of man's existence. We live in an ocean of uncertainty, with waves that never stop coming.

I have discussed change and the fact that many forces are outside of our control. The negative things that befall us can be divided into two kinds: the ones we can fix, and the ones we must accept. But looking deeper -- as our minds are inclined to do -- we want to know: *why* do these bad things happen?

Several years ago, I had what we call a "bad day," full of hard luck and bad news. I met up with a friend in the evening to whine and complain. He was an older friend and listened patiently to me for a while, but as I must have showed no signs of stopping, he finally interrupted me and said, "Tom, you're 35 years old. Why are you still surprised when *shit happens?*"

The question stunned me in its simplicity, and it was something I thought about for some time afterwards.

Later, I came across a passage from Marcus Aurelius: "How ridiculous and strange to be surprised at anything that happens in life." The whole concept was new to me. I had heard many times the phrase that "Life isn't fair," but had never really accepted it.

We are taught as children to "play fair," and children are often heard complaining that "It's not fair!" I commend the worlds of school and sports for endeavoring to operate on a platform of fairness. However, after the relatively "fair" worlds of high school and college, we then enter the real world, which doesn't abide by what is fair and what is not. It is a world where almost anything is possible at any time. Still, we are psychologically not prepared for when a crisis erupts. And when it does, our first question is simple: *Why?*

Two-sided Coins

Author and critic Christopher Hitchens, who himself died of cancer at 62, once wrote, "To the dumb question, 'Why me?', the cosmos barely bothers to return the reply, 'Why not?'" Yet, as said earlier, to ask "why" is to be human; we are all born with curiosity. Our education influences this inquisitiveness, especially in the West, encouraging us to find out why things are they way they are. This inquisitive spirit has been the source of much discovery and also of many triumphs. Can you imagine life *without* curiosity? It is such an inherent part of our natures.

While we do not have hard proof that suffering and tragedy have been with us since the dawn of mankind, we can safely assume that they were as much with us then, as they are now. It is also safe to say that over the millennia, there has been suffering and tragedy for each human in each generation.

Suffering and tragedy have been with us since the dawn of mankind.

Historian Edward Gibbon, writing his monumental *Decline and Fall of the Roman Empire* in the 1700s, described history as "little more than the register of the crimes, follies, and misfortunes of mankind." Gibbon was writing 200 years ago, and about what had happened 2,000 years ago. Seneca adds that "No era in history has ever been free from blame." So bad things, whether by nature or from human conduct, are nothing new. Sadly, they are somehow woven into the texture of living.

Now before that sounds too grim, let's look at the other side of being human – the side that adapts. One aspect of being human, that is slightly amusing, is that we tend to require ourselves to like something before we accept it. We don't handle "unpleasant truths" very well. When it comes to the fact that "shit happens," we have to accept it, but – as with external change -- we certainly don't have to like it. As we develop more peace of mind, the more we can accept the things we cannot change. Whether we like them or not becomes irrelevant to our happiness level.

Curiosity also has its two sides. Aurelius, who lived at the time period that Gibbon focused on in his book, observes that too much curiosity, too much asking of "why?", is pointless. He states,

Like anything else, too much curiosity can be bad for us.

"A cucumber is bitter – throw it away. There are briars in the road – turn aside from them. This is enough. Do not add, 'And why were such things made in the world?'" We seldom think that curiosity can be taken to excess, but it is no different from any other human aspect. Like anything else, too much of it can be bad for us.

WE ARE STILL HUMAN

At the same time, we don't want to go too far with denying a human perspective on what is harmful to us. To react too impassively to tragedy runs the risk of us losing our humanity. The ancient philosopher Anaxagoras, when informed that his son had just died, gave the matter-of-fact reply of "Well, I was aware that my son was mortal." I doubt that any of us would want to develop such a callousness in ourselves, as to have reactions such as this.

A classic text about the crises of life is Harold S. Kushner's *When Bad Things Happen to Good People*. Kushner's motivation to write the book began with a case of personal tragedy: his toddler son was diagnosed with progeria, a terminal disease in which the body ages abnormally fast, causing those who are inflicted to die in their teens. For Kushner, a rabbi, this was particularly hard to accept: he had always been a devout man, and was attentive and respectful to both God and human beings. He was also an educated man and a thinker. Hence, this unwarranted intrusion of suffering into the life of himself, his wife, and his son was something that he could not simply accept without questioning.

Kushner's book, both moving and well-written, gives explanations of how tragedy occurs and why it is a part of our lives. When I read the book the first time, many of these

> *God has designed a world that obeys physical laws without exception.*

were revelations. For me, the most interesting part was when the author discussed how God cannot interfere with laws of nature. God has designed a world that obeys physical laws; these laws do not change to allow for, or pardon, our mistakes and mishaps. As the poet Alexander Pope says in his *Essay on Man*,

> Think we, like some weak prince, th' Eternal Cause,
> Prone for His favorites to reverse His laws? . . .
> When the loose mountain trembles from on high,
> Shall gravitation cease, if you go by?

Let us also not forget that God has given us free will. We have very little control over the actions of others; over most people, we have none. The laws of nature do not change with regard to our unique circumstances. Whether we jump off a cliff, or fall off it, or are *pushed* off it, these physical laws are the same.

The consideration of laws of nature, as well as free will, helps us to see life as more "consistent,", if still somewhat unfair. The laws are the same for everybody, and everyone has free will – and there are good and bad sides to both. But what about the random, unpredictable natural disasters that occur, like hurricanes and earthquakes? Furthermore, what about the unfairness of being born with a terrible disease? And how to explain the presence of animals that can kill us?

There are scientific reasons to explain natural disasters, but the questions will lead to asking why such possibilities have been put on Earth in the first place. In a similar way, medical studies can show why people are born the way they are, looking at such aspects as chromosomes, and other biological factors. But why would these issues be present to begin with? I think that if I were able to ask God one question, it would be, "Why can't everyone at least be born healthy?"

Questions like these cannot be answered, regardless of how diligently we try. They are beyond the scope of any of the gifts we've been given as rational human beings. They will elude us until the end of our existence. Bad things have been happening since time immemorial, and aren't going to stop anytime soon. All we can do is use the best ways of dealing with them, psychologically and emotionally, and in a way that acknowledges our right to be human – unlike Anaxagoras. These include:

- Accepting that it is unreasonable to expect life to be fair

- Acknowledging that life isn't asking you to like what has happened

We are not constructed to bear tragedy on our own.

- Don't expect to get through tragedy by yourself. As we've said before, "No man is an island." We are not constructed to bear tragedy on our own.

- Avoiding the continual asking of "Why?"

- Also accepting that there is no relationship between worrying about surprises and the surprises themselves. All the worrying in the world will not prepare you for unexpected bad things or stop them from happening. All you can do is cope in the best way possible, and the way to do that is to have calmness, the equanimity of peace of mind, as your go-to feeling.

There are a myriad of books on the process of dealing with tragedy and loss, and I do not attempt to cover such an extensive topic here. Our concern here is having the right perspective for being able to move forward – a subject which is reinforced in the next chapter, The Future.

14   THE FUTURE

The notion of anticipating the future is both reasonable and human. The problem is that this anticipation soon turns into chronic worrying. For the anxiety sufferer, a constant fear of what will change in your life can be disastrous, sweeping you into that current of nonstop thinking and negativity.

For many years, and especially during my depression, my life was divided into thinking about the past and the future. The present – which I should have been concerned with -- was completely neglected. While thinking about my past made me depressed and melancholy, thinking about the future inflamed my anxiety and also deepened my depression.

OUR CONCEPT OF THE FUTURE

While Persius says that "We spend our tomorrows worrying about our yesterdays," we also spend a great deal of time in the present stressing about our tomorrows. One reason is that society actually encourages it. Our cynicism as a society, with regard to the future, is reflected in many things, notably in science-fiction films. *Blade Runner*, *The Terminator* and many other films of this genre depict the future of humanity as a dark world, often one in which there has been mass destruction and in which people have lost their individuality and freedom.

Considering all the strides that we have made since the Scientific Revolution, it is ironic that our conception of the future is so negative. What would someone from the year 1700 say if she were to be transported to our time period? Look at all the advantages of living in our Present, which, for her, would be "The Future": methods of transportation, advances in medicine, indoor plumbing, instant access to information, availability of books, education for all social classes. Is "the future" so bad?

We cannot live simultaneously in the past, present, and future. You must choose one. Looking back is never a way to move forward, and the future is useful as a casual guide but not as a home for your thoughts.

> *The future is useful as a casual guide, but not as a home for your thoughts.*

The Western cultures, which are mainly Christian and very linear in their views of existence, tend to have the highest anxiety levels about what will happen in the future. When I lived in Thailand, a Buddhist country, I saw a much lower level of future anxiety, and I have found Buddhist philosophy to have a calming effect.

BEING FUTURE-OBSESSED

There are those that live their entire lives in the future, always planning, thinking, worrying about what will take place, essentially wishing that they were somewhere – or "sometime" – else. During my teens, when I lived almost entirely in the future, only thinking about colleges and jobs and material success, someone told me about a passage she had come across, which has since become well-known:

> *When I was in high school, I was dying to graduate and get to college. When I was in college, I was dying to graduate and get a job. When I got a job, I was dying to get married and buy a house. When I was married, I was dying to have kids, and when I had kids, I was dying for them to grow up and get married and have kids themselves, so I could be a grandmother.*
>
> *Now I'm really dying -- and I realize that I've never lived.*

You only truly live when you are focused on the Present.

What this passage says, is that you only truly live when you are focused on the present. The past and the future are tunnels, blocking out the light with which a focus on the present can enrich your life.

"What If?"

Life inevitably involves taking some chances.

Many people live their lives with the "What If?" principle. I have been one of them. There is a constant feeling of "What if I get old and cannot retire,"

"What if I buy a house and the property values drop," etc. These are serious concerns, no doubt, but does it do you any good to keep thinking about them, again and again? Overthinking is never a solution to anything, and the constant turning over in the mind of the same subject will cause frustration and confusion.

In cases where you are worried about something of this nature, take caution – carefully, prudently, advisedly. But do not be paralyzed by thought. In the case of retirement, talk to a financial consultant. If it is a case of not having enough money, put yourself on a path to earn or save more. Of course this is easier said than done. Most things in life, that are worth doing, sound easier than they are. You start by breaking them down into parts, and doing them one by one. In the case of property values, as mentioned above, talk to an expert, get as much information as you can, and then make a decision. Unfortunately, the future is not going to magically reveal itself. Life inevitably involves taking some chances.

FREE WILL AND RANDOMNESS

And there are reasons for this. The world consists of two main elements: randomness and free will. Despite all the physical laws of the world, and despite the gifts of Reason, Logic, and Science, there is still a lack of perfection with which the world works. As discussed in the last chapter, natural disasters and freak accidents show us that the Earth is not a perfectly regulated place. The senseless murders and other acts of violence, the irresponsible and selfish abuse of money by the financial industry, show us that free will is indeed part of our world. Because these are random and variable, we cannot predict them.

Free will seems to be part of God's plan – whatever that plan is – so it is something we must also accept. As for the randomness, I venture to say that it is a byproduct of creating a natural world. If God starts to prevent avalanches, earthquakes, and hurricanes, where does this involvement stop?

Because of the inherent randomness of the natural world, and free will, God doesn't know the future. If he could see it, and you believe in an all-loving God, he would be unable to stop himself from intervening. And intervention, for whatever reason, is something God will not do.

PREPARING FOR THE FUTURE

The past is something we cannot change; the future is something we do not know. Yet while we cannot control what happens to us, we can make ourselves as prepared as possible. You may recall what I have said about personal change: although we cannot control the fact that external forces change, we can certainly make changes to ourselves. Living your life in a way that contributes to your mental and physical health in the present, such as keeping fit and constantly learning, will help you stay prepared for the future.

I have referred to the ability to compartmentalize. Schedule times at which to concretely focus on what is likely to happen in your future, rather than pondering what may happen and exhausting yourself. This means, in your professional life, updating your resume once a month in case a better job comes along. Physically, it means having annual or biannual medical and dental checkups, to prevent anything bad from getting worse. On the relationship side, it may mean setting aside time every few months to sit down with your spouse and have a candid talk about how you have been feeling and about what is and isn't working. The most important thing is to take action on the things that are actionable, and to accept that the other things will happen as they happen.

As I've said before, no one is asking you to *like* the bad things. Life is going to throw everything at you, good and bad. Happiness is not found in the things that you get; rather, happiness is something that you develop, and eventually, you are happy because of what you have become. The more positive you start to think and act now, about yourself and your life, the more comfortable you will be about the future, and the further you will be on your path to happiness.

15 <u>PERFECTIONISM</u>

Most, if not all, of us failed the first time we tried things in our early childhood. Walking, crawling, eating, even using the bathroom. And then we conquered them. So why doesn't an understanding of this formula of "Failure preceding success" stay with us into adulthood?

I was often told by people, "You're a perfectionist," with a smile, as though it were a positive attribute. In fact, perfectionism leads to catastrophizing things, as well as inactivity, complaining, and a fear of failure, all of which make any type of success impossible. It has a terrible effect on confidence and creates an aversion to attempting new challenges. To be confident and successful, and to lead a life that does not become a process of boxing yourself into a very limited existence year after year, you have to accept that you won't be perfect.

We are taught from our youth that we should strive for perfection. In many ways, this acts as a motivator during our school days. Getting "100%" on a test, or straight A's on your report card, is something children strive for, and which their parents and friends are proud of.

Unfortunately, when we get out into the real world, we still retain this belief that perfection is attainable, unaware that the world is a much less regulated place than school. Real life involves things going wrong, people not fulfilling their obligations, sickness, and simply bad luck – hopefully not all together (though that sometimes happens).

Nevertheless, it's amazing how influential our childhood experiences can be: Having been taught that we can be perfect, we still demand perfection from ourselves, and are surprised when we can't attain it.

Naturally, there's nothing wrong with trying to "Be all that you can be," as the U.S. Army says. The problem is that we often confuse "doing your best" with being perfect – denying the simple fact

> *When you demand superhuman results, you are setting yourself up for disappointment.*

that perfection is not part of the human experience. When you expect and demand superhuman results from yourself, you are setting yourself up for disappointment, and even worse realities than that.

I've included some lessons below that show the perils of perfectionism, as well as some further advice to remember next time you want to beat yourself up for losing a deal, making a mistake, or just not being the perfect machine you think you should be.

BEN FRANKLIN'S QUEST

Ben Franklin, whom I've often referred to in this book, attempted the quest for perfection. In his *Autobiography*, which is great reading for anyone looking for self-improvement, he describes an experiment he made with perfection when he was still a young man. Franklin took 13 rules of conduct, which he called "Virtues," and tried to enforce them in his personal life.

The virtues consisted of avoiding too much alcohol, working hard, sincerity, and frugality, among others. Franklin actually kept a notebook where he daily recorded instances where he broke these rules. Talk about a perfectionist!

Despite Franklin's most diligent efforts – and he is indeed a symbol of hard work – he found perfection impossible to attain. He was able to master some of the virtues, but one of them, "Order," gave him an immense amount of trouble. In "Order," Franklin required that everything be done at the proper time, with no distractions or surprises.

Naturally, we can all see the problem with this expectation. To have complete "order" means that the world around you has to obey your exact will and schedule. In time, Franklin learned to disregard this demand for perfect order, as that type of regularity is simply not written into the DNA of life.

FATALLY FLAWLESS

Tal Ben-Shahar talks convincingly about the perils of perfectionism in his books *Happier* and *Being Happy*. The latter actually has the subtitle, "You don't need to be perfect to lead a richer, happier life."

In *Happier*, Ben-Shahar gives an example of perfectionism that is much more grim than that of Franklin. He tells the story of an Oxford student and scholar, Alasdaire Clayre, who had reached the heights in his field. In addition to top honors and accomplishments at one of the most elite universities in the world, Clayre also wrote a novel and made two music albums, constantly demanding more than the best from himself.

Clayre's television series on China, which he wrote and produced, won an Emmy award. Nonetheless, he only viewed his achievements as rungs on a ladder leading to perfection. When Clayre realized that he could never reach this unattainable zenith, he took his own life, while still in his 40s, and with so much still to offer the world.

This is definitely an extreme example. However, while most perfectionists do not kill themselves, they often kill their own happiness and that of those around them, as well as stunt the development of their talents.

PERFECTIONISM MEANS PARALYSIS

The worst byproducts of perfectionism are the development of inaction and fear. As Ben-Shahar states, "Perfectionism means paralysis." The continual pressure that you give yourself to accomplish absolutely everything, to be free of flaws, makes you unable to act, for fear that the result will not be what you wanted.

As a writer, and someone who works with writers, I see many examples of how perfectionism is self-destructive.

Writers with great ideas are afraid to put the pen to paper, for fear that the result will not be exactly what they desired. Others continually tear up and rewrite their manuscripts, with the view that their next book will be perfect. The result, of course, is that there are no "results" at all — their books never get published!

And then there are those who do go ahead, but get such unrealistic expectations for themselves that they are never happy: the salesman who cannot accept failing to close a potential client, or the entrepreneur who beats herself up when one of her projects doesn't work out.

This fear of failure is also present in our non-working lives, in a myriad of ways. "Fear of Public Speaking" is constantly rated one of the top fears among people, and the reason is that people are worried that they will get up in front of a group and make an embarrassing mistake, or that others will look at them and make a negative assessment. When I was a young man, I feared having my first sexual encounter, and after it finally happened, was so critical of my own performance that I actually apologized to the young lady and swore I would never have sex again. Fortunately I gave it another chance! But it took some time to get my courage back.

Perfectionism and anxiety have a close friendship. As you become more aware of the presence of perfectionism in your thinking, you will see how closely related it is to anxiety. Perfectionism and anxiety are connected, and form a vicious backwards sequence that results in inaction. Those who suffer from anxiety must be on their guard against a perfectionist streak, and vice versa.

"ACCEPTING" THE BEST

To achieve perfection, you would have to live in a perfect world: one without conflict or natural disasters, and where people were never late, sick, or wrong. In short, a place where people weren't human. When you force yourself to be perfect, you also demand perfection from others. Is this fair?

Releasing yourself from perfectionism begins with looking at the world around you. Whether or not it is a beautiful world is debatable, but no matter how positive you are, you will admit that it is certainly not perfect. Knowing this will help you to take a realistic look at yourself as well.

In my junior year of high school, I had to take my SATs. At the time, the highest possible score was 1600. As a perfectionist, naturally I wanted to achieve the full score. I had started preparing for the SATs over a year in advance, with special books, and even took a private SAT preparation course. Hence, you can imagine my disappointment when I only got a 1360 score.

My reaction, in keeping with the person that I was at the time, was to be morose and bitter, and I spent much of my summer studying to

We often confuse "doing your best" with being perfect.

retake the test again in the Fall. I put in 100% and then took the test, and it went pretty smoothly. When I got my result, a 1430, the principal of the school called me out of class to shake my hand. I also knew that although I hadn't received a 1600, a 1430 was going to be my maximum. While this was not a "fact," as no one can see the future, it was a feeling deep inside that I knew to be true. My scores would be good enough for almost any college. Was I happy? I knew it was my best, and I was able to accept that I wasn't perfect.

Sometimes, the simplest solutions are the best. At one stage during my career as a salesman, I had several months of really good sales, and got to the point where I really thought I could have a month where I closed 100% of my leads. When this of course didn't happen, I complained about it to my sales manager, who was an older and much wiser man. He simply said, "Tom, you can't win 'em all" – and he was right.

So, strive to win, and push yourself to the optimum. But when things don't work out, keep in mind that none of us can be perfect, and that we don't live in a perfect world. "To make no mistakes is not in the power of man," says Plutarch, an author who studied the lives of renowned Greeks and Romans. The phrase "You can only do your best" is something to be taken literally.

Finally, when aiming for your "best," make sure it is a goal that challenges you and which doesn't make you miserable. As mentioned earlier, you have to enjoy the journey as well as the destination -- or else you end up with a Pyrrhic victory.

16 STRENGTHENING THE CORE

Several years ago, I started to hit the gym harder and train for greater muscle mass. I was powerlifting, enlarging my shoulders and especially my arms, and eating ravenously, just to put on more muscle. I was getting in better shape – or so I thought. For some reason, my body just didn't feel good. I was constantly in pain, sore, and feeling like I was carrying heavy bags on my back (even though I wasn't). The biggest blow came when I injured my lower back and had to see several specialist doctors.

Ultimately, after a few diagnoses, a doctor told me something that has stuck with me for the past few years and made me much happier – mentally as well as physically. He said that while my exercises were building my "peripherals," i.e. my arms, they were not strengthening my core, which had become at risk from all the heavy weights. The core muscles are in the neck, abdominals, lower back, and buttocks (the "glutes"). In short, while I was building up the parts on the outskirts of my body, I was ignoring and weakening the parts that were essential.

I've seen a similar phenomenon happen with the way that people live their lives — particularly those who are ambitious in their professions. They continually add more "weight" onto their lives, in the forms of more staff, more projects, and more small companies. At the same time, they increasingly ignore the core elements which have made them strong in the first place. When this happens, they and their work start to spin out of control or just gradually lose steam.

So let's look at these core "muscles" of the ambitious professional:

HEALTH

> *The healthy man has a million wishes; the sick man has ONE.*

I was once told by an older friend that "The healthy man has a million wishes; the sick man has one." Indeed, our health enables us to work and to enjoy life. Unfortunately, health is the thing that we are most likely to take for granted. Going through the day and eating one meal, sleeping for 4 hours, and getting little or no exercise means that you are ignoring your core health needs. There's lots to say on what constitutes a healthy regimen for a busy person, but for now, a minimum of 6 hours sleep, at least two regular meals, and some form of walking or cardio three times a week are absolutely required.

BEING ORGANIZED

As busy professional, you don't need to be reminded of the importance of efficiency and streamlining. But the Excel sheets and unanswered emails do pile up, even in our digital age. In some ways, our age is worse, as we don't physically see how much of a backlog we have. So, strengthen your core by putting all of your spreadsheets in order, eliminating duplicates, getting back to people who didn't seem immediately important, and dealing with any hiring (or firing) decisions. Take a morning or afternoon and delete all the computer files that you haven't opened for a few years. Emails that are over 6 months old can be deleted or archived. If you have a messy desk, take an hour and make the desk bare except for your laptop, a pen, and a small notebook.

CORDIALITY

No doubt that no matter how cutthroat and ruthless you can be, you also have good people skills; otherwise, you wouldn't have made it this far. In your devotion to getting ahead, the importance of giving people the time with you that they deserve may be slipping. Make sure to remind yourself how important it is to make each person you deal with — whether clients or colleagues — feel important and valued.

TIME MANAGEMENT

This includes learning to say "No" to potential projects, simply because you don't have the time, energy, or resources to manage them successfully. As with my weightlifting program, I had to take a step back and make sure that my body had regained its core strengths before moving on to heavier weight; to refuse to do this, would be to exacerbate the condition of my back. True, the thought of money being at the end of a tunnel is difficult to resist, but you need to guard against a mental and physical overload or the drawbacks will outweigh the benefits.

"Core" Benefits

I saw the importance of core strengths and their revitalizing qualities when the last doctor told me to take a Pilates class. I didn't know quite what to expect at first, but as the doc said it would be good for my core, I agreed.

It was a small class. After the first lesson, my instructor approached me with a stern look and said that I was "off-balance" and "stiff." She was certainly right. My posture was bad, but worst of all, she said that I was "top-heavy" – that my core muscles, especially in the lower back and glutes, weren't strong enough to support the upper body, where I'd spent all my time exercising and building.

> *We often spend too much time building, while neglecting our foundations.*

Again, I saw a direct correlation to many of us who overwork -- who spend such a great deal of time building and building, but who, in their pursuit of being in excellent financial "shape," neglect their foundations.

I took my instructor's advice, and devoted more time to my own physical foundations. I still wanted to go to the gym to build the "peripherals," but since I only had a limited amount of time and energy, I decreased the weight training and went to the Pilates classes instead. One aspect of the sessions that I really enjoyed was that strengthening my core created a feeling of "flow", of the body and mind being in harmony. (An excellent book on "flow" is by Mihaly Csikszentmihalyi, and is simply titled *Flow*.)

ONE STEP BACK, TWO STEPS FORWARD

After a few months, my back had significantly healed, and overall I felt physically much better, without all the pain or soreness. And yes, I went back to lifting weights and found that despite not trying the heavy stuff for a few months, I was actually *stronger* and able to lift more — most importantly, without the pain and unpleasantness.

You will find that the same is true in the non-physical part of your life. Letting your kids' extracurricular activities run your life, cluttering your private time with too many engagements,

> *Taking one step back enables us to take two steps forward.*

overworking without a focus – it is not hard to find examples of what to change. Simply put, sometimes you need to slow down for a short time in order to become better. Again, as Thoreau said, "Simplify!"

17   LIFE'S MEANING

Life is indeed a bizarre thing. We can't see the future, we can't change the past, we have to work to live, we have to work hard to *find* work, and ultimately, regardless of how much we learn or experience, we don't even know why we are here. In the saying "Truth is stranger than fiction," we should really be substituting "truth" with "Life."

For many years, I woke up asking God for the meaning of life. The "answer", if there was one, was that he was never going to tell me. Somehow, knowing this would make things too easy. We have to find it or make it for ourselves. Indeed this is not fair, and I would even say that it is not logical. But Life and Reason are two different things.

Viktor E. Frankl, in his book *Man's Search for Meaning*, tells the story of his Holocaust experience and offers his views on the meaning of life, as both a psychologist and philosopher. He states that "It is impossible to define the meaning of life in a general way," and adds that "Questions about the meaning of life can never be answered by sweeping statements."

Whenever I am asked what I think the meaning of life is, my answer is always the same: "We aren't meant to know."

It is not the perfect answer, nor the one that anyone is looking for, but to me it is the only possible answer. To know the meaning of life would be to explain all the other mysteries of life. It would

> *We aren't meant to know the meaning of life.*

be like a decoder, as the Rosetta Stone did with hieroglyphics. For whatever reason, we're not supposed to know what it is.

CLASH WITH HISTORY

Human history, despite Edward Gibbon's quote about it being a register of mankind's follies, has largely been a history of discovery. The fact that we do not know the meaning of life does not "fit in" with this pattern. Science, philosophy, mathematics – all have had a progression from ignorance to knowledge. At the same time, we are not one step closer to identifying why we are here.

We have no concept of a world without Time. We have no concept of a world not being *created*, but just *being*. Likewise, if life has a meaning, it is something that is beyond our grasp as humans. We have investigated science to the point that we know the universe was once an infinitesimal ball that exploded. But we don't know why it exploded, or who put it there.

The elusiveness of life's meaning sometimes feels like a cruel joke, especially on days when we are feeling down. We are tempted to ask why we are even bothering to remain alive. "What's the point?" we may ask. But we also have to accept that there must be some reason behind our existence. Would someone create something as complex as Earth and the universe, as well as something as complex as human beings, for no reason?

Human Nature

We have talked about asking "Why?", and I first started asking "Why am I here?" when I was in my teens. It was the time when a young person first starts to feel stress about the future.

Children seem to be immune from feeling curious about life's meaning; despite their inquisitiveness about nearly everything, they don't question Life. One can assume that they are glad enough just to be living it. The time when we start to question things is in our teens, when we become aware that we will be expected to support ourselves for many years in the future. Suddenly, existence becomes a kind of burden.

I have discussed "why" several times, and the fact is that as humans, there really is no escaping it. With the spectrum of qualities that we are born with, curiosity is one of them. Surprisingly, we are prone to question the meaning of life but not to question other profound aspects of our lives. Why do we want children? Why do we want relationships? Why do we want success, power, and money?

Questioning the meaning of life inevitably leads to thinking about God and the afterlife. Thinking of Heaven can be a great inspiration to lead a life that is upstanding and honest.

At the same time, I have never been able to form a rational conception of how heaven works. The questions abound: What if some of our friends don't make it there? Do we have good

> *Heaven, like life, is beyond the scope of human reasoning.*

days and bad days? Do we have neighbors who are noisy? And how does living a "good" life for 70 or so years earn you paradise for eternity? Heaven, like life, is beyond the scope of human reasoning.

DERIVING MEANING

Russian author Leo Tolstoy's short story *The Death of Ivan Ilych* relates the concept of finding meaning in life through relationships, through caring for others. The story depicts the life of a man, Ivan, who is selfish, concerned with material possessions, and uninterested in other people aside from how they can advance his career. He becomes physically ill from an obscure abdominal disease, which symbolically reflects the disease of his mind -- that he has never found any real meaning in life, or for his life itself. It is a "long" short story, and while reading it, we too become weary with feeling Ivan's emptiness. Despite not liking Ivan, we empathize with him.

At the end of the story, Ivan is in bed, writhing in pain, dying, as his poor peasant servant is lifting his legs to make him feel better. Ilych sees the happiness in the boy's face – the boy's happiness in helping another -- and exclaims, "It's beautiful!" He finally realizes what could have given his life meaning, and passes away.

The story corresponds with a section of Frankl's book, in which Frankl identifies three ways through which we can find meaning in life. The first is our work, whether it is our job itself or a special pursuit like scientific research or philosophy. Second, is the "love" side of our lives: relationships, family, and friends. Third is suffering. "Sometimes even to live is an act of courage," says Seneca, and Frankl's experience shows how this courage becomes deeply meaningful. Frankl suffered in a concentration camp, though there are plenty of types of suffering through which we can derive meaning: disease, the deaths of loved ones, miserable poverty. Through all of these, we can discover a dignity in ourselves, which helps us to see meaning in being alive.

In my case, I didn't discover what gave my life meaning until the end of my depression. I was only in my late 30s, but I had made a lifetime's worth of mistakes, and I realized that the meaning of my life was to serve as a warning and lesson to others. In time, I expanded upon this, and ultimately my life's meaning is found in helping others to develop peace of mind and happiness.

Seneca, who like Marcus Aurelius (and myself) sees life as a war, observes the meaningfulness in pushing forward against the difficulties presented by life: "And yet life is really a battle. For this reason those who are tossed about at sea, who proceed uphill and downhill over toilsome crags and rocks, who go on campaigns that bring the greatest danger, are heroes and front-rank fighters."

Practical Prescriptions

We live in a world where traditions are looked upon with contempt, where most of us do not live simply to survive, and hence people are wondering what they are living *for*.

On days when you are down, and are questioning the meaning of life, keep in mind that there are also a large number of beautiful things that have been given to us. I've already talked about making a list of the things you like, and which you are thankful for. The list will not lead you to life's meaning, but it will illustrate to you the positive aspects of being alive. Focusing on these positive things will help you fight negativity. Remember that *the first step is always a change in perspective*.

Further, accept that life's meaning is unknowable. Constantly pondering life's meaning is not a way to enjoy life. Spend your energy and time on the things you

> *Instead of focusing on life's meaning, focus on what gives YOUR life meaning.*

can control, and on the things you can change – including yourself. Instead of focusing on life's meaning, focus on what gives *your* life meaning. Focus on what is meaningful to *you*, regardless of what the meaning of life is as a whole.

18 PRIDE

The word "pride," and its adjective "proud," have taken on diverse meanings over the centuries. In our age, it is common to hear the word used positively, as in "I am proud of my daughter – she is first in her class at school." Of the words that comprise what were called the "seven deadly sins" – lust, greed, wrath, pride, sloth, gluttony, and envy – it is only Pride that has acquired a positive connotation.

Pride is often used to mean a sort of self-appreciation, but here, I use it in its original sense – that of excessive regard for oneself and a selfish and arrogant sense of dignity. The dangers of pride do not lie in appreciating your achievements. Rather, pride is harmful because it endangers your ability to succeed, both personally and professionally. Pride renders you unable to take criticism, unable to take orders, and hence unable to deal with reality.

> *As pride comes from within, so it must be defeated from within.*

As pride comes from within, so it must be defeated from within. For most of my life I had a "pride problem," even though I thought I was humble. The fact was that I was only humble when it suited me – which is not really being "humble" at all.

A MASTER OF DECEPTION

For those who suffer from pride, life will be one long painful lesson in humility. Life does not like proud people. And hence we have the saying, "Pride comes before a fall." In my case, life knocked me down

> *For those who suffer from pride, life will be one long painful lesson in humility.*

again and again, though I didn't change my sense of pride. It was not until I examined the causes of my falls, rather than the events themselves, that I realized I had a serious pride problem. All of the humiliation in the world cannot destroy pride on its own; it is something that, as it is inborn, you have to address yourself.

Pride is an excess of confidence, i.e. arrogance. The Greeks had a word for the type of pride that is self-destructive, which they called "hubris." It is unfortunately a word that is no longer part of common speech, as it is useful in capturing how pride leads us to delusions which are harmful to others and to ourselves. In Asia, this sense of groundless, uncompromising pride is found in the concept of "Face." Having lived in the Far East for 15 years, I can safely say that this concept is responsible for a lot of bad decisions and problems.

When you make decisions based on your pride, you are not thinking rationally or clearly. You are prioritizing yourself over Reason and over others. Indeed, pride is a master of deception. Pride also encourages the "all or nothing" approach: "It's my way or the highway." Pride congeals with many things to make them worse – fatigue, failure, fear. I had a bad mixture of anxiety (fear of the unknown) and pride. It resulted in me losing my temper far too often.

Pride does not pay bills. As such, pride is also an enormous obstacle to success. As a salesman, what hindered me most from enjoying my job and succeeding was that I didn't like people telling me "No." Who did I think I was? God? Of course people are going to tell you "No," just as you are free to say "No" to others. Successful salespeople do not allow themselves to be stepped on, but they know that being proud will get in the way of business. As one of my friends puts it, "Pride does not pay bills."

A LIFE LESSON

Suppressing one's pride is not easy, and in my case, I asked for help from above. God gave me an interesting lesson. My family wanted to go on an important trip to see our ancestral roots, and frankly I could not afford to go. I stressed and stressed about this trip, how it would severely damage my finances, though my pride would not allow me to tell them. Finally, with the figures of flight costs and hotels staring me in the face, push came to shove, and I had to tell them I wouldn't be going.

This was a lesson in pride, that pride cannot change certain realities. But the lesson continued. My father wrote back and said that the trip was really important to the family, and that he and my mother would pay for my expenses. My initial, gut feeling was to refuse. I didn't like people to pay for things for me – after all, I had my pride. But what actual *benefit* was I actually getting out of my pride here? This was what I pondered.

I had to choose: to stick with my pride and say "No," which would have hurt everyone involved (including me, as I really wanted to go); or to say "Yes," swallow my pride, and make everyone -- including myself -- happy. I have always been very independent, and have taken great pride in my independence. I thought I needed no one, and Life proved me wrong again and again. This, here, was my introduction to seeing how helpful it could be if I suppressed my pride. I said "Yes," and we had a wonderful trip.

"Be not ashamed to be helped," says Marcus Aurelius, "for it is thy business to do thy duty like a soldier in the assault on a town. If you are lame, you cannot mount up on the battlements alone, but with the help of another."

MANAGING PRIDE

Pride is one of the more difficult aspects of character to control. It is very psychological. Nevertheless, here are methods that have worked for me, when I am feeling prideful:

- Think about how much you dislike it when others make a decision based on pride.

- Look at the full context, the bigger picture: how does this situation damage your well-being, aside from your pride?

Great people know how to swallow their pride.

Think of great leaders, and how often they must swallow their pride to get things done. Surely you admire bosses who take your suggestions, and who are willing to change their minds if they are wrong.

- Remember that pride goes against Wisdom, and that the latter is something that we all want more of. We'll talk more about Wisdom in a later chapter.

- Finally, no one has ever attributed either their success or happiness to pride. It is an obstacle to both.

As mentioned, pride is a difficult character trait to manage, and it will take time. View each instance of overcoming pride as a victory, and as a step on the road to greater clarity.

19 LUCK AND CHANCE

Chance is like change – it is written into the DNA of life. It is the kind of change that cannot be foreseen or explained.

The human race has taken great strides to dominate Chance: the studies of probability and statistics, and our tendency to refer to "the odds," whether in sports or in everyday life. But we forget that the essence of chance is that it cannot be predicted or completely understood, and that it is always present – not simply a study which begins and ends with a textbook.

ANALYZING LUCK

It is easy to be cynical about luck. When we see others being lucky, we forget that luck is random. We take luck very personally, and often give it human characteristics, attributing it with being responsible for our situation.

While luck is indeed completely random, this also does not mean that it is distributed evenly. Probability would say that over an infinite period of time, everyone would have the same amount of good luck and bad luck; but over limited periods, as in a casino, one can have almost purely one kind of luck. This implies that there are people in life who are lucky over and over again, and whom luck seems to "favor." Some may call it Destiny, some may explain it as random chance being predisposed in their favor.

Nevertheless, I have never heard of anyone who became successful simply by being lucky. Some intelligence is needed to get there. An actor or athlete on the rise, regardless of luck, can destroy his career by making racist comments or an act of extreme violence. Even lottery winners have the courage, or the imagination, to go buy a ticket.

Likewise, there are instances of good luck that seem favored by Nature from the beginning. Some people are lucky to know from an early age what to do with their lives. Some people are born rich. Some people are born with very athletic genes. We can ponder this till we drive ourselves mad, or we can pay attention to our own lives. We can focus on what we *can* control.

> *It is easy to attribute another's success to luck, because it frees us from self-blame.*

It is easy to attribute another's success to luck, because it frees us from self-blame. Since luck cannot be controlled, it is easy to say to ourselves that the only difference between us and that "lucky" person is a stroke of fortune. I disagree with this. Sure, there is an element of luck in the circumstances surrounding one's birth. This may be debatable, but I would argue that it is better to be born to a financially comfortable family than a poor one. It is certainly better to be born healthy than not. And, when we are fetuses, we have no control whatsoever over the conditions in which we are born. So yes, some people are luckier than others right from the outset. There are also issues of intelligence and IQ, physical stature, and aesthetics.

Nevertheless, none of these "lucky" circumstances are absolute requirements in order to reach peace of mind and happiness. You do not need to be born rich, or with an IQ of 170, or with genes that will make you a shoo-in for a basketball career. This book was inspired by the fact that I was born with anxiety issues and depressive tendencies, and I have proven to myself that these are not obstacles to a happy and fulfilling life.

"PREPARING" FOR LUCK

This brings me to a perspective which I have held for some time, that *Luck is something we can prepare for, but not expect.* While we cannot predict whether we will be lucky – or unlucky – we can make sure that we have built ourselves up to be ready for it.

> *Luck is something we can prepare for, but not expect.*

Many people will talk about a successful person's "lucky break," not considering the state that person was in when the break arrived. I've known several businessmen over the years who seemed lucky: someone came to them with an opportunity at the right time, they stumbled (or even fell) into an industry that became "hot," they were in the right country or region that started developing. When you look deeper, you see that luck was only able to play its role because these people were prepared for it.

As an example, I offer a businessman I know personally. In the early 1990s, the U.S. was affected with the "cigar craze," as cigars once again became popular among a mass audience. It matched the strong economy at the time. Entrepreneurs began opening tobacco shops, and my friend, who already had a shop, began to make some very substantial profits. Customers and onlookers would say, "Wow, how lucky for him that there is this cigar craze – he's really in the right place at the right time."

Few knew, however, that he had started that shop with his wife in 1980 and given it the utmost attention over the years, while earning a very modest profit. During that period, he treated that shop with the attention of a father, investing countless hours in making sure that it was in excellent condition. Cigars need to be humidified at a certain rate and temperature, and he invested in a state-of-the-art system to make sure this was done right. Hence, when the cigar craze came, he was 100% ready. When patrons would tell him he was lucky to be in the right place at the right time, he would smile and say, "Yes, we had 14 years until our 'overnight' success."

The same is true of many of my friends who became successful in China over the past decade. While many expatriates treated their China experience as a long vacation, others spent the time investing in themselves – learning the language and the culture, and studying the economy. They even took the chance of starting businesses. When good luck arrived, they were prepared for it.

In a similar vein, the year of my life where I had the most luck and financial success was the year where I had the most positive attitude, as well as the most self-discipline and work ethic. True, I was in the right industry at the right time -- which was lucky -- but I would have made nothing out of this luck if I had not been prepared.

These are examples of professional luck, but the same carries over into our personal lives. For us to be lucky to meet the right partner, we need to have invested in ourselves to some degree. Generally we need to be gainfully employed and relatively healthy, and with a positive perspective on life. To hear about a good deal on a house or car, we need to have friends and connections who could share such information, and the financial soundness to understand this information.

Preparing for bad luck follows the same formula. We prepare for losing a job or other financial adversity by making sure we save

Preparing for whether Fortune smiles or frowns upon you follows essentially the same guidelines.

some of our salary each month. We prepare for catching a cold by taking care of our health, such that the effect of the germ is minimized. So much in life can be handled with relative smoothness, if we just acknowledge that good and bad luck will happen unpredictably, and that while we cannot be totally prepared, we can at least have the best foundation possible to deal with it.

We are all dealt different hands in life. We can sit around cursing our bad luck, and questioning until we make ourselves confused as well as unhappy, or we can resolve to be as prepared as possible for what may happen to us. Being prepared for whether Fortune smiles or frowns upon you follows essentially the same guidelines:

- Spend as much time as possible with your loved ones

- Have savings, and do your best to be re-employable, like learning more

- Maintain your health – a little self-denial now is better than a lot of regret later – and have insurance

- Keep a positive attitude, such that you do not repel opportunities

As you see, these preparations are extremely simple. I am often asked, "What if we prepare and nothing lucky follows?" Then at least you have improved yourself mentally and physically. Nothing wrong with that, right?

We're Luckier than We Think

There's nothing strange about being thankful for a day in which nothing went wrong.

Have you ever tried flipping the concept of luck upside down, and thinking about how *unlucky* you could be? From the moment we wake up in the morning, can you imagine the things that *could* go wrong, but don't? It is perhaps not a comforting thought at first, but ultimately it helps us to see the improbability of bad luck and the fact that things usually go the way we want them to. Don't forget to include this in your feelings of gratitude. There's nothing strange about being thankful for a day in which nothing went wrong.

THE LAW OF ATTRACTION

Much has been said over the last fifteen years about the Law of Attraction and the use of the subconscious in determining what happens in one's life. This was popularized by the film called *The Secret*, which I have watched several times.

I have mixed feelings over what is expressed in *The Secret* and in the Law of Attraction literature that has been proliferated as a result. The main fault that I find is the total disregard that the Law has for the presence of randomness in the universe. This law states that anything that happens to us is a direct result of our thinking, or of our subconscious. Such a notion is absurd, especially when one considers natural disasters such as earthquakes and tornadoes. No one brings these upon themselves, no matter what they may be thinking about. The same applies to someone who is hit by a speeding drunk driver. There is nothing you can do to "attract" something like that. It simply occurs as a result of the free will of someone who acts irresponsibly.

As for the power of the subconscious, the books on the topic tend to give vague descriptions of how to use this power to bring about greater success. There is no tangible path, nor are there any precise methods. According to these writings on the subconscious, thinking about something repeatedly, to make it happen, seems as equally helpful as *not* thinking about it and just letting it "be" in your mind. The messages are contradictory.

The only consistent message of the Law of Attraction, and the notion of the subconscious, is that it is important to be positive, and that generally good things happen to positive people. The more you clear your mind of negativity, the more favorable things can happen. We still cannot control the effects of the universe's randomness, or most of the actions of others. Don't delude yourself into thinking that an avalanche is your fault.

20   <u>LEARNING</u>

Learning helps us to be happy. The mind derives pleasure, and a sense of confidence and purpose, from knowing new things. I know very few (if any) happy people who have ever stopped learning. And I have seen happy and successful people act with great humility in order to learn from someone who can teach them something valuable. Why do students tend to be happy people? Partly because they are learning -- not just because of parties and a relative lack of stress.

The notion that "Where ignorance is bliss, 'tis folly to be wise" (from a poem by Thomas Gray), is a romantic notion of ignorance – one of smiling simpletons working

> *No one wins a battle through ignorance, and certainly not the fight to be happy.*

in a field. It ignores the reality that ignorance is where people are weak and can be deceived. No one wins a battle through ignorance, and certainly not the fight to be happy.

FACILITATING THE PATH TO HAPPINESS

One of my constant questions in life has been, "Why do so many things need to be learned the hard way?" Despite all the years we have of school,

> *Experience is the most painful path to wisdom.*

we really aren't taught much about life. One may argue that we are taught how to think, but I am of the view that a great deal of wisdom about life is still reserved for being learned through experience – the most painful path to wisdom.

"As long as you live, keep learning how to live," says Seneca, for "No man was ever wise by chance." What has always surprised me is the sheer absence of courses on Wisdom, and even the absence of Wisdom sections in bookstores. There are indeed "Philosophy" sections, but I think of Wisdom as the practical side of philosophy, not esoteric arguments couched in convoluted language. One would think that there would be Wisdom sections of bookstores so vast that eventually there would be stores entirely devoted to selling books on Wisdom.

Inexplicably, there aren't. Wisdom remains something that we need to seek out and find. It also remains something, paradoxically, which we have to judge for ourselves.

The challenges here are considerable. The people in our immediate lives who have the most wisdom, our grandparents, generally die when we are young, and before we appreciate and recognize how much we can learn from them. Western culture emphasizes independence at an early age – which I'll admit does have some benefits – but one of the drawbacks is that it makes us resistant to learning from our parents. Schools focus on subjects that are academic but largely unrelated to real life. When I finished high school, I knew how to do calculus but not how to write a check. The university system is guilty of the same.

I have spoken of confrontation, and that we shy away from it because of fear. Learning gives us the knowledge to overcome these fears,

> *Learning increases our ability to overcome fear.*

and to take charge of situations. We did this all throughout our early childhood. Never stop.

So How Can We Continue to Learn?

View knowledge as something you can acquire, not as something you don't have. That is, look at it positively. It is a matter of perspective. There are many ways to keep learning, even as an adult. There's no shortage of inexpensive or convenient ways to learn. There are community colleges, online courses, and DVDs of Harvard courses, as well as the *Dummies* series of textbooks – just to name a few.

We are blessed to live in an age where knowledge is at our fingertips. The internet enables us to read books, order books, and to have access to information that would have formerly taken great amounts of time, energy, and money to acquire.

At the same time, we must use a great deal of self-discipline with the internet, as there is plenty of material online that is not instructive or helpful. Just as junk food isn't good for the body, so is "junk internet" harmful to the mind. Would you feed your body junk food, and nothing else, for years, months, or even weeks on end? No. Then don't do it with your brain. Studies show that wealthy people read at least one book a month on how to improve their lives, and that these books are about business and health.

During my depression, I had trouble reading. It was difficult to focus, with so much going on in my head, and also due to my hedonistic notion that it was easier to go out and party. When I began reducing the hedonism, and waking up in the early morning with a clearer head, I found that I was able to read more without my mind wandering. Initially, I had to slow down in order to become a better reader. As I developed more peace of mind, and more positivity, I found that I was able to read more attentively and for longer periods of time. The happier you become, the more you will be able to read, as your mind will have less anxiety and distractions.

A mental euphoria arises from learning, especially when it is something practical. Years ago, I decided to study Chinese, especially as I was living in China. I sat down for a Chinese lesson and realized that it was the first time in several years that I had actually learned anything new. Even one lesson gave me a rush of cerebral energy. Learning gives us knowledge and also makes us feel younger.

As stated earlier, having older friends is also a very good way to learn. Western society makes it very difficult to have friends who are older, largely because of social constructs and a prejudice against older people. This is something about our culture which needs to change. It is from older friends that you will acquire wisdom in addition to knowledge.

Knowledge is not the answer to every problem. No matter how much we learn, we can't expect to have an immediate answer to everything, and some problems don't have immediate solutions. Wisdom teaches us to have patience. As is said in *The Teaching of Buddha*, "The wise man learns to meet the changing circumstances of life with an equitable spirit."

21   Jealousy and Revenge

In this chapter I illustrate how to deal with jealousy and revenge through life-examples of both. The two feelings are different, yet spring from the same source: human nature. Both also cause resentment, leading to negativity and unhappiness.

Jealousy

Jealousy is among the most natural of human emotions.

Jealousy is as human and fundamental an emotion as anger, happiness, or sadness, yet we do not treat it nearly as seriously. Jealousy is one of the ugly consequences of the Darwinian need to compete with our fellow man. Envy and jealousy (I will use the terms interchangeably), in addition to being human emotions, are also only truly experienced towards other humans. A colleague used to joke that he was jealous of a cat, for its "glorious life of eating and sleeping." However, true jealousy is felt towards another person – someone, for example, who is successful, who has outperformed us, or whose life we believe is just "better" than ours.

As a basic human trait, jealousy – like humans – is an example of imperfection. It blinds us to the reality that everyone's life consists of imperfections; that no matter how ideal one's life looks from the outside, there will always be some things not to envy. Remember: whatever we are here for on this Earth, perfection is not part of it.

Oscar Wilde's *The Picture of Dorian Gray* is a famous tale of the destructiveness of vice and hedonism. Interestingly, it is centered on a young man's envy of *himself* – of a splendid painting of himself, which he laments will stay young and fresh while he grows old. While he gains his wish to have this reversed, the painting starts to reveal his inner wickedness and unhappiness. Dorian realizes that eternal physical youth is not an automatic ticket to being happy. Late in the book, as his friendships and relationships have crumbled, and his life has lost meaning, he says that despite his wealth and youth, he would gladly trade places with anyone, due to his misery. He starts to envy even those he had looked down upon.

I mention this because many of us often have a desire to "trade places" with someone that we know. We may be jealous of them, or simply resent them. I once met a friend of a friend who had just moved to the city, and who was becoming part of our circle of friends, and I realized that I was very jealous of him. In every respect, he was my superior: more successful, more intelligent, more cultured, in better shape, and even an inch taller! My way of "handling" it was to avoid being around him as much as possible. In doing so, I neglected to realize that his life, like everyone's lives, surely had its problems; but I was allowing my jealousy to dictate my actions.

True, it is okay to be human, and jealousy is an inescapable part of our humanity. At the same time, we have the power to control it. I finally asked myself, "Is my behavior fair?" Moreover, was it *nice*? Certainly not. And, putting myself in his shoes, I would not want someone treating me that way, just because he perceived me as being "better." Bearing all of these things in mind helped me to overcome this jealousy.

When you are feeling full of envy/jealousy:

- Accept that it is a natural feeling and that you are not perfect. Don't be ashamed.

- At the same time, keep it to yourself. There's no need to tell others.

- Be conscious of your actions towards this person. Negative thoughts can transfer themselves into actions, even subtle actions, very quickly.

- Put yourself in the shoes of the other person, and remember to "Do unto others as you would have them do unto you." This will help you to erode any resentment arising from jealousy.

- Lastly, keep in mind that no one's life is perfect, and also that there are people out there who would be jealous of *you*, too.

Revenge

But what about the people who harm us? Like jealousy, the desire for revenge is a primal human emotion that is extremely powerful. There is a wealth of movies that carry revenge as a theme, and it can be found plentifully in the world of books, perhaps most famously as the driving theme in Dumas' *The Count of Monte Cristo*.

The feeling of revenge also springs from our Darwinian condition, as we feel that the person who has wronged us has "won." Like it or not, life is competitive. This produces many excellent things, such as cures for diseases, inventions, and the arts. But again, the ugly flip side is the desire to avenge ourselves on those who have "beaten" us in one way or another.

A Mild but Revealing Example

During my depression, I had a few instances where I felt the passion for revenge (though not in a violent way). My only true experience with actually accomplishing vengeance sticks clearly in my mind, and took place during my sales days. Briefly, it involved getting a difficult and rather rude personal assistant in trouble with her boss, to the extent that the latter called me to apologize for her behavior. I nearly danced into my own boss's office the next day to congratulate myself, and distinctly remember saying that I found this feeling of revenge to be "better than sex."

My boss, who was an older and much wiser man, was not at all amused, and he gave me a stern lecture about how foolish I was being. He also seemed disappointed in me. Later, I realized why. Revenge is a primal human notion and is perhaps linked to the basic human mandate to survive, as seen in primitive, prehistoric times. However, since the development of communities, it is a notion that chiefly does harm. And the most harm it does is to oneself. My boss was disgusted with my "celebrating," because in my euphoria over someone else's suffering, I looked ugly and horrific. Who wants someone like *that* to be working for them? The concept of revenge makes a good theme for movies, but people who are bent on revenge are not happy, and certainly not at peace.

LETTING IT GO

I kept this in mind months later, when I was going for an interview for a new job that I was very excited and passionate about. I'd looked forward to it for weeks, and had already imagined my new life with this job. To make a long story short, the manager who interviewed me may have been having a bad day, but whatever the case, he was very dismissive and seemed determined to prevent me from "selling" myself properly. As I left the interview, I felt disappointed, but even worse, I felt humiliated. And as for him, who was a department director with a massive salary, and who would forget my existence immediately and continue to live well, I don't mind saying that I was full of resentment.

I could have easily contacted the head of the company, whom I knew through the Chamber of Commerce -- but something stopped me. I looked at the situation without emotion. True, talking to the manager's boss might get him in a bit of trouble, but it didn't help my situation in any way. Having seen this person, I certainly didn't want to work under him, so the only "revenge" would be getting him a slight reprimand, if that. The time and energy I would spend on that – negative energy – could be spent doing much more positive things.

So I suppressed my feelings of revenge. However, I still felt a huge amount of resentment. Resentment is connected to revenge like sarcasm is connected to anger. I tried telling myself that this person clearly wasn't happy, that he would someday slip up and offend the wrong person, etc. But some of these people who wrong us *are* happy, at least in their own way. Why is it so difficult for us to "let it go"? And is it really healthy for us to hope for someone to fail?

The reason it is so hard to let it go, is because over time, that resentment becomes part of you. Consciously or unconsciously, you may feel that it provides you

> *Over time, resentment can become part of your character.*

with motivation, a source for self-pity, or an explanation for not achieving a certain goal. In a strange sense of the word, it becomes an "asset."

As for the second question above, I am reminded of a quote that has been attributed to several people, including actress Carrie Fisher: "Resentment is like taking poison and waiting for the other person to die." Resentment is really just another form of negativity, which infects the conscious and subconscious.

Always remember that having resentment is like carrying a backpack around that is full of heavy weight. It really only succeeds in slowing you down, or completely bringing you down. Resentment may not go away immediately, but reminding yourself that it is a negative and unproductive force is the big step in dismissing it from your mind.

FORGIVENESS

The concept of resentment has been further complicated by the notion of forgiveness. We hear the Christian doctrine to forgive, or the hyperbole of "turning the other cheek," and often reprimand ourselves for not being able to do it. The word "forgive" sometimes carries an overtone of brevity, as if we should instantly ignore or forget an injury that has been done to us.

What is not said, is that forgiveness takes time. On any scale of judgment, we are human. We are programmed to resent injuries, as they interfere with our innate desires to survive and to be happy. One is reminded of the words of Alexander Pope: "To err is human; to forgive, divine." Forgiveness represents one of the more difficult things for us, as humans, to do.

Forgive people for your own sake, not for theirs.

I am not arguing against the idea of forgiveness. Rather, what I am arguing is that with time, forgiveness is possible, and that it is also necessary for us to have happier lives. A proactive attitude has to be taken towards viewing resentment as detrimental to ourselves. The notion of forgiveness tends to focus too much on the person being forgiven -- who often has not done anything to warrant it --rather than the forgiver. Instead, focus on the resentment itself and what it is doing to you. Forgive people for your own sake, not for theirs.

What I did in the case above, with the interviewer, was sit down and think about how all of this resentment was affecting my mood, how much time and energy I was wasting on it. It was self-destructive. In short, I gradually forgave this person, as a duty to *myself* and my own happiness.

This was a case of short-term resentment, which is easier to overcome. Long-term resentment, which has been nourished over many years, is more difficult. I am reminded of an instance that happened to me not too long ago. In Junior High school there was a classmate who bullied me and made my life very unhappy at the time, causing me ultimately to lose friends in addition to losing my self-esteem. This person was responsible for a lot of the problems I had in my early teenage years, and certainly contributed to a negative outlook on life and humanity that I used to have.

Several years ago – over twenty years after we finished Junior High – he called me, quite out of the blue, to apologize. It was quite a shock.

While I accepted his apology over the phone, my initial reaction was not relief, but rather a feeling that I had been "robbed" of a resentment that I felt justified in having. After all the misery that he had caused me, it now seemed that he was also taking away my right to have it. However, as I looked at the situation over the following days, I realized that there was nothing more to resent. The person I disliked was no longer the same person; but more broadly, I focused on the fact that there could be nothing gained from negative emotions. The situation made me realize that I should have forgiven him years ago – if not for his sake, then definitely for my own.

ONE FINAL NOTE

During my depression, I also began to resent happy people, especially those who seemed to be *born* happy. They are almost always upbeat, positive, looking at the bright side, taking things in stride, accepting change. There is a temptation to resent such people, but the last thing we want to do is resent those who exemplify what we should be trying to be. If you know one of these people, stay close to him or her. People like this stop the world from sinking.

22 <u>PEACE OF MIND</u>

The world we live in encourages us to be happy, but gives us little advice on how to find happiness. This same world also tells us little, or nothing, about peace of mind.

Expecting happiness without first developing peace of mind, is like trying to build levels on a building without a foundation, or expecting branches to grow on a tree without a trunk. A

> *Expecting happiness without first developing peace of mind, is like trying to build levels on a building without a foundation.*

feeling of long-term happiness is not possible without first having a core of composure.

SIGNIFICANCE

When I use the term "peace of mind," I am not referring to a temporary feeling, as with sitting and chanting "om" in a yoga class. Peace of mind is the ability to encounter the unforeseen adversities of life without panic. It is the ability to think and act without an excess of emotion -- a state of self-control, equanimity, and freedom from constant anxiety. It is the foundation for anyone who wishes to be happy, and it is a quality that is more consistent than happiness.

Peace of mind, like happiness, is something that you develop, not simply find. The quest begins with acknowledging that peace of mind is a status to be desired; that it is just as important as happiness, and that it is also a prerequisite for someone who wants to be happy. Peace of mind provides a stability, a traction, that happiness does not. Regardless of how positive your perspective may be, it is not possible to be happy all the time. It is, however, possible to have constant peace of mind -- that traction that enables us to maintain our emotional and psychological stability in the face of difficulties.

> *For those who suffer from anxiety and depression, peace of mind is the Holy Grail.*

For those who suffer from anxiety and depression, peace of mind is the Holy Grail. It represents the serenity to accept the things we cannot change, such as the past, as well as the courage and wisdom to deal with the present and the future. It is freedom from the paralyzing effects of being worried, self-hateful, reflective, overthinking, and the other elements that have brought you down psychologically. As James Allen writes, "To live continually in thoughts of ill-will, cynicism, suspicion, and envy, is to be confined in a self-made prison-hole." Peace of mind is your vindication from this prison.

THE LAW OF SUBTRACTION

> *Simplifying your life is the first step towards acquiring peace of mind.*

"Out of clutter, find simplicity," said Albert Einstein – someone, ironically, who is famous for the complexity of his theories.

To attain more peace of mind and happiness, you must go back to basics, as with the chapter on "Strengthening Your Core." Simplifying your life is the first step to acquiring peace of mind. As you may be in a state of negativity, the presence of greater complications in your life will be proportional to how negative you are. The more complications, the more negativity. It is time to strip down your life, to correct or improve the essential elements, and to then build it back up again on this new foundation.

I call this the "Law of Subtraction." The term does not have a pleasant ring to it, as it implies losing something. Our lives are so focused on "addition," on accumulation and building, that we have a negative view of subtraction, of things becoming "less." But the more we add on to a weak foundation, the more likely we are to experience a collapse.

Writing a century before Einstein, Thoreau, who lived alone in a cabin in the Massachusetts woods, wrote that "Our life is frittered away by detail . . . Simplify, simplify!" It is no coincidence that during the height of my depression, my life was very "top-heavy" with false urgencies that I had allowed to build up. I often got involved with too many activities, and found myself unable to refuse invitations. The effect was that I was constantly rushing from one place to another, fighting city traffic, worried about being late, and then having to leave early for another appointment. In many ways, I was using this complexity as a distraction from healing the core problems of my life -- and these problems were a lack of peace of mind and a dislike for positive thinking.

I was also constantly bothered by outside circumstances, far more than they deserved. Loud noises sent me into a rage; even the sound of a phone ringing drove me crazy. I catastrophized everything. I was already so "on edge" that anything that happened caused me to lose my emotional stability. Naturally, in a world of constant change, this was a serious problem. And instead of making it my own responsibility to find peace, I expected everything around me to give me peace instead.

As discussed, while we live in a world of change, that is no guarantee that the circumstances around you are going to change when you want them to – or that they will change in the *way* you want them to. Any type of change for your self-improvement needs to be initiated by *you*. And hence I had to take those first steps to secure peace of mind, or it would never have happened.

I began by curtailing my lifestyle. Sunday mornings became exclusively for *me*. Evenings from Monday to Wednesday were not for socializing, but either for work, reading, or errands like buying groceries. My whole life needed to slow down, because I was off-balance, slipping and becoming more negative, descending further into the tunnel vision of negativity. This whole process of simplification was really an act of rebalancing, and gaining a foundation.

Be mindful that external circumstances will always play a part in your life. We cannot escape them completely. Even if you are Thoreau and living in the woods, you will be faced with some of the unpleasant surprises that life throws at us. Extreme weather, waking up with a cold or fever, not having a meal to eat – life can surprise us in infinite ways. Nonetheless, we want to minimize this as much as we can.

As you simplify your life, your mind will start to achieve clarity. You will have less anxiety, and you will become comfortable at home or in your "sanctuary," discussed earlier.

> *Each step away from overthinking is a step towards peace of mind.*

As this new sense of comfort begins, you will overthink less. And each step away from overthinking is a step towards peace of mind.

A DOOR TO LEARNING

Peace of mind facilitates a myriad of things, especially learning. It provides the clarity that is necessary for self-betterment.

In the years of my life where I was depressed and full of anxiety, my brain did not absorb new material, nor did I make much of an effort. For one, I had a cynical attitude, which is never good for acquiring knowledge, and two, the time spent learning would detract from the time I would spend on hedonism – that false happiness which is empty and fleeting. Thirdly, if you have a poor attitude about learning, your brain stops *trying* to learn. It is that strange relationship between the technical part of the brain, that "machine" part, and the part that is more personal and human. The two are in constant communication.

Proper praying

While writing this book, I had a colleague in the Philippines who was always at peace and full of life – indeed, a walking embodiment of sunshine. I finally asked her, "How do you achieve this?" Her response was simple and immediate: "Prayer." She added that she prayed every morning, sometimes alone and sometimes with her family, and that this process of expressing gratitude, as well as any hopes, concerns, and penances, put her in the frame of mind to face the day with composure and positivity.

Prayer should mainly consist of gratitude. Be thankful for your family, your health, your job (if you don't like your job, be thankful for at least having a means of earning money). Be thankful for regular meals, clothing, shelter, and for any moments of peace and happiness you have experienced during the day.

It is natural, in prayer, to ask for help. No one makes it through life completely on their own. At the same time, while there is no exact science for praying, it is important to keep in mind that God is not a "genie." Often, people turn their prayers into a Wish List. I was guilty of this in my youth, and would say prayers like "God, make me the best football player in the world" – excusable because of my childish innocence, but definitely not the kind of prayer that is going to get much of a response. Instead, we want to ask for *help* in moving towards an achievement – not the achievement itself.

Ask God for the strength, the confidence, the endurance that you need; ask God to help you see things clearly and positively; ask God to help you make the best use of opportunities that come your way, and to not be overwhelmed by procrastination and fear. As I got to a more peaceful and happier plane, I began to look at my procrastination problem, and saw that it was either a result of perfectionism or the following course: ignorance of what to do; anxiety about that ignorance; a reaction that was prideful or shameful (the two come full-circle); then negativity; and finally, inaction and quitting.

Each day, say the prayer that sums it all up: "God, please grant me the serenity to accept the things I cannot change, the courage to change the things I can, and the wisdom to know the difference."

This prayer covers the main areas of living a peaceful, happy, fulfilled life. Serenity is the feeling of being at peace, which Allen describes as "the fruitage of the soul . . . As precious as wisdom, more to be desired than gold." Courage is the ability to move forward and make the most of opportunities, without letting fear paralyze you. Wisdom, we know, is the use of good judgment and the effective application of knowledge. Asking God for wisdom helps you to avoid learning everything the hard way.

One prayer I often said during my depression, when I recognized where I was and started to gain some focus, was "Please don't let me hurt the ones I love." (I always say "please" when I'm praying.) I didn't want, in my negative state, to bring pain to those around me through my complaining or my anger; and this prayer was answered. While I did not put up a façade around people, I knew how to manage my words and actions so as to take their feelings into account. God helped me to consider the feelings of others, in a way that I had never done before, and I also became a less selfish person in the process.

In your prayers, don't be afraid to be self-deprecating, and to talk about your shortcomings. If you can't tell God, who *can* you tell? I've consistently asked God to help me live with equanimity, courage and wisdom, and to also help me suppress and remove the pride, sarcasm, and hedonism, which had proven to be so destructive to my life. When I started saying these prayers, I also started to notice when I was being prideful and sarcastic, and also when I was allowing hedonistic tendencies to control me.

A very valuable byproduct of prayer is that it is also a way of letting your mind ventilate, like journaling. It is a way of finding a moment of tranquility.

There are many books written on religion, and hence I shall confine myself to just some brief comments here. In keeping with my views on prayer, I believe that there can be great solace acquired through religion. The key is to look for how it speaks to you personally. Religion still speaks to us in platitudes: "God loves you," "Jesus died for our sins" (the meaning of which is not clear), But people are more educated now and are not consoled by such trite statements. They do not feel reassurance from them.

Without going into too much depth, I believe that the best kind of religion is that which helps you in both this life and the next. Religion should assist you, educate you, in getting on a path that helps you to face each day – not just eternity. If a religion is solely focused on the afterlife, it's not doing its job. Elements that a religion should teach, which are often neglected, include:

- How to be frugal and save money

- How to maintain good health and a strong body

- How to take a practical approach to dealing with adversity

- Emotional control and self-discipline

- Keeping an active mind and constantly learning

Yes, it's important to save the soul, but let's not forget about improving the mind and body.

Just a final note on peace of mind: Like anything else worth having, peace of mind is not attained overnight. Make it a constant goal for each day, and you will find that it becomes more of a way of life. Simplify, pray, learn, and exercise, and you will find yourself on the path to equanimity.

23 CONFIDENCE AND MOTIVATION

To the anxiety sufferer, depressive, or negativist, "confidence" automatically means "*over*confidence," or arrogance. We worry that confidence will cause us to act foolishly or offensively. But confidence also means, to us, an absence of worry and fear, which is something we find impossible to comprehend, and something we fear in itself. We fear that confidence will blind us to reality and danger.

Confidence is essential to happiness because it enables us to put our positivity into motion. At the heart of confidence is a positive outlook. Negativity and confidence do not mix, but a positive outlook enables confidence to exist.

Confidence and fear are not mutually exclusive. In contrast to the notion that confidence represents the absence of fear, confidence and fear are not mutually exclusive. You can be confident and still be afraid, and fear is a natural and often logical feeling. If people simply had blind confidence, blind courage, they would be fools -- not heroes. To reiterate a quote from Tal Ben-Shahar, "Courage is about having fear and going ahead anyway."

TYPES OF CONFIDENCE

There are many types of confidence: professional, romantic, social. We experience a clash with social confidence when we are young. In my case, I used to be very concerned that everyone would "like" me. I was nervous in social situations, especially ones involving people I hadn't met, as I wanted to make sure to be liked. Even walking into a bar or restaurant was uncomfortable, as there were many strangers there. I wanted to make sure they'd like me, and I would stress about how I should act.

Having everyone like you is as impossible as having every customer buy from you, and as I got older, I realized this plainly. You can't please all the people all the time, and furthermore, some human beings are simply hateful and negative. Your social confidence should come from the knowledge that you are fair and kind to people. Thankfully, as people get older, they become more mature and are more disposed to appreciate these values.

Romantic confidence is a complicated issue, which is addressed in a wealth of books. For now, I will just say that the happier you are with yourself and with being alive – which is the aim of this book – the more confident you will be in your romantic life.

As we get into our 30s and then middle age, professional confidence becomes critically important. It is linked to success, which is one of the ways we measure how well we are doing in life, and it also relates to how we survive our tough lives as workers. A lack of professional confidence can be a serious problem, whether one is interacting with clients or colleagues. In my case, during the height of my anxiety and negativity, I feared getting new assignments, as I was afraid I would not be able to do them. This fear of failure led to a perception that I didn't want to work or that I was "bureaucratic" in rigidly confining myself only to certain tasks.

In time, I realized that this feeling of mine was really the Fear of the Unknown. We often speak of the "unknown" in solemn terms, but it is not just something grand and mysterious, like life after death. It can be getting a request from a colleague or client and not knowing what do to. The panic quickly turns to resentment: "Why are you giving me this? Why are you leading me to failure?"

Confidence and knowledge are connected. The confidence to do a job often rests on your knowledge of what you have to do. Unfortunately in life, we get requests to do many things that we haven't learned. Other challenges, such as fighting, are less formidable if we know how to fight.

However, you can be confident without having the exact knowledge required, just by knowing that you are *capable* of acquiring that knowledge. For many years, my reaction, when given a new task that I didn't know how to handle, was to panic, think of all the obstacles (or create them), and ultimately make myself miserable. The fact that I was a perfectionist, afraid of making any mistake, only made things worse. And this lack of confidence was visible to others, making them less confident in me.

My lack of confidence got to such a degree that I would look at each task as the final one, with the feeling that once I got it over with, I was done forever. It was the type of self-delusion that one experiences during depression. And then I recalled the story of Sisyphus, a mythological Greek king who was condemned to Hell, with a punishment that he would have to roll an immense boulder to the top of a hill, only to watch it roll back down, repeating this action forever. Each time, he believes it will be the last time, but is continually disappointed.

To look at each task as the final one, or as getting something over with, is to condemn yourself to the same delusional thinking as Sisyphus. There is always going to be another hurdle, another challenge. So how can we approach these nonstop challenges with confidence?

- Learn: Knowledge increases confidence. A boxer does not get into the ring with an opponent without training heavily beforehand. The same goes for any profession. We live in a world where you can order a book on any profession and have it delivered to you digitally within seconds. When you fear the unknown, make it less unknown by learning about it.

- Avoid perfectionism: The paralyzing effects of perfectionism also apply to confidence. Confident *Confident people do not expect to do anything perfectly.* people do not expect to do anything perfectly.

- Break things down into parts: Most projects or assignments, however overwhelming when looked at as a whole, are composed of much simpler components. My favorite story on this regards a British acquaintance from my China days whose business was setting up private schools in China. China is notorious for bureaucracy, as everything has to be approved by the Communist Party -- especially in the education field. I asked the man about how he dealt with the already formidable task of setting up schools, coupled with the red tape of the government, and I really liked his reply. He said, "There's about 560 things you need to do to set up a school in China. Some are easy, some are hard. So you just make a list of those 560 things and go through them, one by one." In other words, you don't get emotional or take it personally – you just get to work. This applies to life itself, which is really just one big project, composed of many parts.

- Don't deny your former triumphs: You should derive confidence from the fact that you have succeeded in challenges before. And as these experiences have enriched you, they make you even more capable now to face the next challenge.

- Lastly, put things into perspective: Fear causes us to magnify the difficulty of things. As with everything in life, don't overthink.

HAVING A "PLAN B" -- DOES IT HELP?

I had always thought that one way of staying happy and comfortable was to have a Plan B, and if possible a Plan C, at least as far as work was concerned. "What would happen if I lost my job *today*?", I often asked myself.

What I didn't realize, was that by investing all this time in thinking about Plan B and Plan C, I was taking time away from investing in Plan A, i.e. my current job. Also, it's likely that I may have even been giving the impression, though unknowingly, that my current job was not satisfying me.

For many successful people, there never was a Plan B. I asked a friend of mine who invested all he had in a business, and who emerged successfully, what his options would have been if things had not gone well. "There wasn't another option," he said frankly. "I never even thought about it."

Nonetheless, a Plan B can be beneficial, as long as it does not detract emotionally from your Plan A. Otherwise, you fall into a "grass is always greener on the other side of the fence" situation. Yes, keep your CV up to date, and don't be afraid to listen when someone mentions a possible opportunity. But keep your focus on what is in front of you.

TAKING RISKS

To someone with a negative view on things, and also suffering from anxiety, the notion of taking risks seems absurd. Nonetheless, the more confident you become, the more natural it will be to take risks. Ben Franklin says that "there are no gains without pains," and this applies to risk, as there are few gains without taking some type of risk – whether that involves applying for a new job, taking a course, investing in a stock or property, or even entering a relationship.

> *If you cannot take risks, you will never feel free.*

If you fail, you learn and move on. The only way to prevent failure is to take no risks, and this means taking no steps to improve your situation. If you cannot take risks, you will never feel free.

But What About Failure and My Self-confidence?

Let me relate a little story here. In my late 20s, I was an up-and-coming publishing salesman in Shanghai, and increasingly confident. When I got approached by a different firm to start a new magazine, I accepted the opportunity. For the next year, I worked twice as hard as I'd been working before, and saw few results. Customers just simply weren't interested. And when the magazine closed – failed -- I found myself in a unique situation: all of my confidence had been crushed.

The fact is, I had never been truly "confident." The confidence that I had felt prior to starting the new endeavor was simply related to external circumstances – that is, I was having a good run at sales in my previous job, because it hadn't been such a challenge. Internally, I had no *foundation* of confidence. Thus, when I took a risk and it didn't work out, I was devastated – I had based all of my confidence on external conditions. Was I a good salesman? Did I know what I was doing? I ignored what I felt inside, and only focused on what was outside, blaming myself completely for the magazine's failure.

(Just a final note on this experience: when I later spoke to a consultant about why the magazine hadn't worked out, I was told that the magazine was a good product but in the wrong market. He compared it to selling socks on a South Seas island, where no one wears them. It was one of the most profound lessons in marketing that I've ever learned, and has since helped me immensely, even guiding me against making some poor investments.)

LYING ABOUT CONFIDENCE

Confidence is one of the few things that it is okay to lie about. People don't want to hear that you are cautious or worried; they want to hear that you are confident. By all means, if it is a matter of your own safety, say that you are not confident. However, you will find that brutal honesty about your ability to undertake an assignment or project is detrimental. As an anxiety sufferer, you are inclined to think you cannot do it, and to start seeing and mentally creating obstacles in your path. It takes every ounce of courage, but you should keep these feelings to yourself and try to not think about them. If necessary, write them down rather than express them orally. Then go through them one by one.

Richard Branson has been quoted as saying "If somebody offers you an amazing opportunity but you are not sure you can do it, say 'Yes' – then learn how to do it later." One's first reaction is to say "But what if I *can't* do it?" The reality is that most assignments are not difficult when broken down into parts, and your past successes and accomplishments should reinforce your confidence in getting a new project done. So don't be afraid to lie in these cases, unless there is danger to your life or limb.

The Surge of Capability

By following all the steps above, you will arrive at a state of feeling that I call the Surge of Capability. This is a state where you feel that you can accomplish anything. Harness this feeling and make use of it as often as you can. Never let energy or confidence go to waste.

Motivation

Motivation starts from the beginning of the day. Marcus Aurelius writes, "In the morning, when thou risest unwillingly, let this thought be present—I am rising to the work of a human being. Why then am I dissatisfied if I am going to do the things for which I exist, and for which I was brought into the world?"

His message is simple: we have a responsibility to make the most of ourselves, to maximize what we have been given as human creations. The question arises, however, as to what exactly is supposed to make you motivated. Some people are born with a passion, and others have to live for a while in order to discover theirs. My passion for constantly improving myself and trying to help others was only realized after thirtysomething years, and after many attempts at finding other motivations!

If you haven't yet found something that motivates you, don't panic – it is out there. We are all human, and motivation is part of our genetic

Anxiety and hedonism are threats to motivation.

makeup. But you need to get into a position where you can feel a motivation or inspiration. Anxiety, at its strongest, will instantly dismiss ideas that are motivating; hedonism will crush these ideas, by comparing them with instant gratification. Good things – ideas and opportunities – come to people who can hold on to them, and hence you need to make yourself prepared by finding peace of mind and a positive perspective.

A spirit of motivation also guards against procrastination, which is similar to the paralysis caused by perfectionism. You will notice that there are always plenty of reasons to procrastinate, and the mind comes up with these reasons very easily. It is a sign that the easy things in life are not the things which get us ahead or help us reach our full potential. For some reason, exercise seems to be the easiest action to procrastinate against: the weather is either too hot or too cold – or, if it's just right, why "waste" that weather on exercising? You are too tired, or even too full of energy, to spend it on running or weightlifting; you have too much work, or you finally have free time and want to enjoy it. The list goes on and on. The fact is, you will always be able to find a "reason" not to do something that requires effort. Nike sums it up best: "Just do it!"

When you have found what motivates you, the next hurdle is to be persistent. The more focused you are, and the more positive you are in your thinking, the more persistent you can be. The negative mind thinks up all kinds of reasons to not be persistent, and the mind that overthinks also works against you. The simplicity that we have worked on in this book provides a clarity that helps you to stay persistent, enabling you to keep your "eyes on the prize" and to keep putting your energy into motion. Remember that nothing is perfect, and that in any project or endeavor there will be the smooth parts and the rough parts. Don't let the rough parts make you stop pushing forward.

24 DEVELOPING HAPPINESS

Developing happiness is both a search and a battle.

The search begins by stating to yourself that happiness is possible. This requires courage and also a positive perspective on your life and

Any shortcut to happiness is an ill-chosen route.

the things around you. Unfortunately, as with anything that is worth having, there are no shortcuts. Drugs, alcohol, sex, and other types of hedonism produce a short-term happiness which becomes counterproductive. The reckless spending of money – if one can afford it – offers only a temporary euphoria. Hence, like most shortcuts, any shortcut to happiness is an ill-chosen route.

WHAT DOES "HAPPY" ACTUALLY MEAN?

The word "happy" is used in such a carefree manner in everyday life that it has become hard to define. Dictionaries define it as "feeling or showing pleasure or contentment"; others substitute "joy" and "satisfaction." For a word used so often, it is interesting that the authorities on the language seem only able to define it by using synonyms.

For our purposes, we are not talking about a momentary happiness, as in "I'm happy about the way my meeting went today." When we talk about happiness here, we are using the word to signify a positive outlook on life, which we already accept isn't perfect, and an outlook which is established on the foundations of peace of mind and a positive focus.

The famous essay *Desiderata*, a very uplifting piece about having a positive perspective, ends with the encouraging sentence, "Strive to be happy." For many years, this sentence frustrated me. Why should I have to "strive"? I thought that happiness was something that came to you, something that depended on the way external events were going.

On top of that, the word "happy" lacks a sense of duration. Can we be happy all the time? We certainly cannot be joyous when there is the death of a loved one, or when we are out of work and needing money. In such cases, we are not in much of a mood to "strive to be happy." So what is this phrase supposed to mean?

First, as I have stated throughout this book, being happy is something that you have to fight for. Yes, there are those who are born with a sunny outlook. However, for most of us, that outlook is something that we have to work towards, through all of the means that have been discussed. Physical health, suppressing pride and hedonism, overcoming jealousy, avoiding overthinking, ignoring the past – these are all forces that we fight against as we strive for and develop happiness.

Second, life isn't supposed to be easy. Nor is it supposed to be completely joy-filled. To be happy, you have to accept that happiness is not a constant state. It is more of a general mode, a perspective, rather than a constant feeling. "Happy" people are not bursting with joy *all* the time: they feel tragedy, and they have bad days. The difference is that they have a foundation of peace of mind that does not allow them to lose themselves to violence, as well as a reservoir of positivity that does not allow them to descend into negativity and depression. Being an overall "happy" person means accepting that there are things that will happen in life that are bad, even terrible, but that they don't change your perspective. It is then, and only then, that you can start being a genuinely happy person, not a slave to the moment or a fool in denial.

> *To be happy, you have to accept that happiness is not a constant state.*

Hence, what "strive to be happy" really means is *Use everything in your power to be a positive-thinking person.* Focus on what you can control and change about yourself, clear away the elements that are nonessential, and treat your body with the respect needed to have energy and a lucid mind. Be thankful for all of the positive things you have. Be thankful for the things that you like and love about life.

RESPONDING TO THE MIND

At the beginning of your ascent to being happy, you will feel momentary instances of happiness. When this occurs, say Thank You. It doesn't matter who you thank – God, Life, the Universe, or your mind itself. The important thing is that you are showing your gratitude for this feeling. Don't analyze it. Just enjoy it, be thankful, and don't dwell on it.

Epictetus writes that "There is only one way to happiness, and that is to cease worrying about things which are beyond the power of our will." With all due respect to Epictetus, I find this to be incomplete. First, it is not easy to simply cease worrying; and even when one can achieve this, a cessation of worrying will help bring peace of mind, but not happiness. To achieve the latter, it is necessary to adopt a positive outlook.

For me, the hardest part of developing happiness was my tendency towards rumination and overthinking. When you dissect anything, you find its negative aspects, and I was prone to dissecting *everything*. It made me a good student of literature, but that's about it. And combined with this was a negative groove that I'd become stuck in, all of which severely worsened an inborn anxiety problem. As I've said earlier, I had to rebuild, and this book has been partly an account of my own rebuilding process.

TRAPS

The road to happiness is not an easy one, and here are some "potholes" to avoid:

- Nostalgia: During my depression, I fell into a habit of glorifying the "good old days" of my early 20s, when life was easy. In fact, it wasn't easy; it was just that

I had a life of complete hedonism. And this caught up with me when I was thirty. I gradually discovered that having a life of goals was much more fulfilling.

- Fear: This involves being afraid to be happy, because you fear how you will feel when unhappiness strikes.

- Guilt: Don't let people make you feel guilty for being unhappy. Sadly, some people actually think being happy is as easy as the click of a button. This entire book would not exist if that were so. Some circumstances are difficult to bear, and take time to recover from.

- Cynicism: This is related to the Fear trap. People think, "Why deceive myself by allowing myself to be happy, when I know the world is terrible and I'll just eventually become unhappy again?"

Basing your happiness on externalities: Letting your happiness depend entirely on another person is like basing your happiness on the weather. It can also be seen as selfish. Yet many people do it, and there seems to be an undertow that draws us towards doing it. Never let anything that is out of your control be a basis for your happiness.

> *Never let anything that is out of your control be a basis for your happiness.*

Life Doesn't Give Us All the Same Things

One further reason why it is unwise to base your happiness on external circumstances is that life does not give us all the same things. It is not possible for the entire population of the world to be financially wealthy, or for every person to have a genius IQ, or for each individual to be splendidly athletic. The presence of so many people who have these traits and who are still unhappy testifies to the notion that happiness is not derived solely from what happens outside our minds.

The famous sitcom *Cheers* had a rather understated ending, which depicted this concept of happiness. In the last episode of the show (which ran for 11 seasons), Sam Malone, the lead character, takes stock of his life and thinks of himself as a failure: a lackluster baseball career, one failed relationship after another, and running a bar that struggles to keep afloat. Yet at the end of the episode, and in the last few minutes, he realizes that compared to the true friendships that he has, and the joy that it brings him every day, the other things don't really matter. In the final line that he speaks, as the series comes to an end, he calls himself the luckiest person in the world.

A Pessimist is Not a Realist

One saying goes that *A "pessimist" is what an optimist calls a realist.* The joke implies that optimists do not see reality with the appropriate objectivity. However, bear in mind that there is no such thing as being totally objective. One's perspective is either positive or negative. To be perfectly objective would be superhuman or robotic. We are born with a tendency to interpret things, to mentally digest them, as negative or positive. The "glass half-empty or half-full" is a perfect example. Hence, we have the capacity to choose whether we want to have a positive or negative perspective, and this is a *choice*. As Churchill said, "I am an optimist. It does not seem too much use being anything else."

The pursuit of happiness, as Victor Frankl says, is really a pursuit of a reason to be happy. If you have a positive perspective, you can find that reason. Peace of mind enables you to incubate and nourish and recharge that positive perspective, such that you don't lose control of it when something unpleasant happens.

BEING HAPPY FOR OTHERS

It's not always easy to be happy for others when you are feeling down. Just remember that their happiness does not detract from yours.

> *There is room in the world for all of us to be happy.*

Happiness is not a limited resource, like precious metals or grain or even water. Happiness cannot be owned by another person, nor can it be hoarded or confined. There is room in the world for all of us to be happy.

EPILOGUE

So let us fight the battle . . . and rouse ourselves to
meet the things that attack us.

- Seneca

If you can adhere to the advice given throughout our journey together, you will reach a point where you realize that you are happy with yourself and with life, and where you hope your life never ends. In my case, I was sitting in a cheap restaurant in the Philippines, with the noise of traffic and motorcycles around me, and the relentless heat, but these things didn't matter: I realized that I didn't want to die, but that I loved life, and that I loved my *own* life. It finally happened. And that was the day I started writing this book.

There will be days when you feel as though you are being fought every step of the way. And there will be days that you will glide through. Fight on, knowing that a life of "perfect" happiness exists for no one, but that the guidance given to you during our journey will make the tough days as few as possible. In the fight for happiness, you can be the winner. I know, because it is a fight that I myself have won. If I can win it, so can You.

Lightning Source UK Ltd.
Milton Keynes UK
UKOW04f1844171017
311164UK00001B/5/P

9 781491 784099